THE INCOMPARABLE

# CHRIST

THE INCOMPARABLE

# CHRIST

OUR MASTER AND MODEL

VAUGHN J. FEATHERSTONE

Deseret Book Company
Salt Lake City, Utah

**Library of Congress Cataloging-in-Publication Data**

Featherstone, Vaughn J.
    The incomparable Christ : our master and model / Vaughn J.
Featherstone.
        p.   cm.
    Includes bibliographical references and index.
    ISBN 1-57345-061-8 (hardback)
    1. Jesus Christ—Mormon interpretations. 2. Spiritual life—
Mormon Church. 3. Mormon Church—Doctrines. I. Title.
BX8643.J4F42     1995
232—dc20                                                     95-682
                                                              CIP

Printed in the United States of America

10   9   8   7   6   5   4   3   2

Dedicated to all of the innocent who oftentimes suffer far more
than the guilty—those with wayward children and those
who are hurt by divorce, incest, death, disease,
physical disabilities, unjust criticism,
and much, much more.

I pray and hope they will find peace
and comfort in this book.

# CONTENTS

. . .

# INTRODUCTION

. . .

During general conference in 1950, President Harold B. Lee stated, "It is my conviction that every man who will be called to a high place in this Church will have to pass these tests not devised by human hands, by which our Father numbers them as a united group of leaders willing to follow the prophets of the Living God and be loyal and true as witnesses and exemplars of the truths they teach." (Conference Report, April 1950, p. 101.)

Writing this book has helped me understand the love, mercy, and condescension of our Savior and Lord, Jesus Christ. It has provided personal insight into the eternal consequences of His mission. I have become more aware than ever before who this Jesus really is. I believe I understand more clearly what it means to walk in His steps. The essence and sum of His life consisted of His suffering for others, His serving, healing, weeping, teaching, soothing, loving, enjoying, empowering, and befriending all who walk the earth. He continues to touch our innermost lives as deeply as we individually permit Him. His unconditional love is absolutely void of force, dominion, and compulsion.

Those who choose to let Him become the center of all they are and do will surely be tested. In our own way we tread our individual winepresses, for, as President Lee stated, we will pass through tests not devised by human hands. But we need not do it alone.

Our son Scott recently received word that one of his sons is deaf. This is the third deaf son in his family. I believe this is a test not devised by human hands. Scott and Lori have a wonderful attitude regarding this test: "If God sends us one more *special* child," they say humbly, "we can handle it." They have and they will continue to "handle it"; nonetheless, it is not easy. These three boys, in addition to three more hearing sons, require a tremendous amount of time, finances, and care.

One day as I considered the test this family faces, the following thought came to me. These three boys are young children. Perhaps they will be here when the Savior comes in His glorious return to earth. If they are, perhaps someone will bring to His attention that there are three men from the Featherstone family who are all deaf. I can imagine Him blessing and healing them. In reality, I know that whether this miraculous event occurs is of little eternal consequence, for after the resurrection they will all hear—a later but equally great miracle.

I would gladly give my hearing for any one of these three special boys, but God does not work that way. Each must bear his own burden. I hurt deep inside whenever I think that in this life they will never hear a mother's song, a prophet's voice, laughter, wind, storms, birds, animals, and all the sounds that make up life. They will not hear the wonderful singing of the Tabernacle Choir, the sacred hymns, or the happy music of children laughing.

Yes, we tread our own private winepress, and sometimes it seems to us too great to bear. It is crucial that we then recall the majesty of this Supreme Being, the Only Begotten of the Father, who powerfully declared, "I have trodden the winepress alone," and we realize that it truly was alone. This book is an attempt to put into words the love, reverence, commitment, dedication, and loyalty to Christ that I feel deeply in my soul. I thank my God daily that His "charity never faileth."

PART ONE

. . .

# OUR MASTER

CHAPTER ONE

· · ·

# Holiness to the Lord

The season of the world before us will be like no other in the history of mankind. Satan will unleash every evil scheme, every vile perversion ever known to man in any generation. Just as this dispensation of the fulness of times brought the restoration of all that is good and holy, so also did it bring the fulness of evil. As parents, spouses, children, and members of Christ's church, we must find safety. Unfortunately, many will struggle mightily before recognizing this bitter truth: *there is no safety in this world*—wealth cannot provide it, enforcement agencies cannot ensure it, even membership in the Church will not guarantee it.

As the evil night darkens on this generation, we must come to the temple for light and safety. Only in the house of the Lord will we find quiet, sacred havens where the storm cannot penetrate. There unseen sentinels watch over us. So it was that the Prophet Joseph pled with God during the dedicatory prayer of the Kirtland Temple: "And we ask thee, Holy Father, that thy servants may go forth from this house [temple] armed with thy power and that thy name may be upon them . . . and thine angels have charge over them." (D&C 109:22.) The Lord has promised: "I will go before your face. I will be on your right hand and on your left, and my Spirit shall be in your hearts, and mine angels round about you, to bear you up." (D&C 84:88.) Surely angelic attendants guard the temples of the Most High God. It is my conviction that as it was in the days of Elisha, so it will be for us: "Fear not: for they that be with us are more than they that be with them." (2 Kings 6:16.)

Before the Savior comes the world will darken. The time will come when even the elect will begin to lose hope if they do not come often to the temples. I believe that the Saints will come to the temples not only to do vicarious work but also to find a God-given haven of peace. True and faithful Latter-day Saints the world over will long to bring their children to the temple for service and for safety.

The Lord has promised that He will "suddenly come to [His] temple." (D&C 36:8.) "The day or the hour no man knoweth; but it surely shall come." (D&C 39:21.) We need to prepare for that day.

There are those among our youth today who will be someday called to the holy apostleship. The rest of us are walking with them daily, unaware that one day God will move His hand and the mantle of apostleship will rest upon them. We must keep those who have been so foreordained sweet, clean, and pure in our wicked world. Mothers will cradle in their arms and nurse at their bosoms babes who will yet become God's living oracles.

There are great unseen hosts in the temple. Joseph told the brethren, "And I beheld the temple was filled with angels." (*History of the Church*, 2:428.) I believe deceased prophets of all dispensations visit the temples. Those who attend the temple will feel their strength and companionship. We will not be alone in the house of the Lord.

Faithful, endowed members of the Church who keep all their covenants and properly wear their sacred coverings will be safe as if protected behind temple walls. The covenants and ordinances are filled with faith as a living fire. In a day of desolating sickness, scorched earth, barren wastes, sickening plagues, disease, destruction, and death (see Joel 2:2–6; also D&C 29 and 133), we as a people will rest in the shade of trees. We will drink from the cooling fountains. We will abide in places of refuge from the storm. We will mount up as on eagles' wings; we will be lifted out of a wicked, insane, and evil world. We will be as fair as the sun and clear as the moon.

The Savior will come and honor His people. Those who are prepared and therefore spared on that glorious, triumphant day will be a temple-loving people. They will know Him and see Him "red in his apparel, and his garments like him that treadeth in the wine-vat. . . . The sun shall hide his face in shame, and the moon shall withhold its light, and the stars shall be hurled from their places." The redeemed "shall mention the loving kindness of their Lord, and all that he has bestowed upon them according to his goodness." (D&C 133:48–49, 52.) They will cry out, "Blessed be the name of he that cometh in the name of the Lord. . . . Thou art my God, and I will praise thee: thou art my God, I will exalt thee." (Psalm 118:26, 28.) Then we will all join in one grand hosanna that will ring from one end of eternity to the other, a hosanna shout to God and the Lamb.

Those who live in that day—whether that be us, our children, our children's children, or some future generation—will bow down at His feet and worship Him as the Lord of lords, King of kings. They will bathe His feet with their tears, and He will weep and bless them for having suffered through some of the greatest trials ever known to man. His bowels will be filled with compassion, His heart will swell wide as eternity, and He will love them as no mortal can love. He will bring peace that will last a thousand years, and they who have become his children of the covenant will dwell with Him.

Let us prepare this special future generation with faith to surmount every trial and every condition. We will do it in our holy, sacred temples. Come, oh, come up to the temples of the Lord and walk in His edifices wherein there is truly "holiness to the Lord."

The Lord's temples stand as ensigns to the nations. They tower upward as monuments to our Master and Savior. All that we do in the temples ties to the Atonement. I thank God for His grand and holy temples. I thank God for the light, knowledge, and instruction that distills upon me and all who attend the temple in faith. May we praise His holy name forever. May we always be inclined toward His holy purposes, and may God watch over and have mercy on all who faithfully perform the glorious work as saviors on Mount Zion. Oh, how beautiful are the feet, the robes, the countenances, the souls of those who come to the holy temples of God!

## CHAPTER TWO

# Justice According to the
# Supreme Goodness of God

I have thought much about the topic of justice according to the supreme goodness of God. (See Alma 12:32.) Not surprisingly, I have discovered that God's justice is centered on the Savior's atonement. The Atonement was wrought for our sins. "The blood of Jesus Christ . . . cleanseth us from all sin," wrote the Apostle John. (1 John 1:7.) The Atonement was the greatest act in time or in eternity by any mortal soul who has ever walked this earth. Through the Atonement the lost shall be saved, the prisoner shall go free, the burdened will receive peace. All that is required of us to receive this wonderful gift of God is to repent.

All my life I have spoken of and been grateful for mercy. Mercy is an act of incomprehensible and never-ending charity. Mercy must of necessity be extended into the lives of all who would be partakers of divine forgiveness of their sins and trans-gressions. As a General Authority, I have witnessed mercy being extended through many wonderful experiences.

In Alma 42:24 we read: "For behold, justice exerciseth all his demands, and also mercy claimeth all which is her own; and thus, none but the truly penitent are saved." Note that justice exerciseth *his* own, and mercy claimeth all which is *her* own. It is interesting that we give daughters names like Mercy, Faith, Hope, and Charity, whereas sons are named after justice, such as Justin or Justus.

Recently I developed an appreciation for justice that is as profound and precious as my feelings for mercy. Justice is an eternal principle and must be satisfied. It is equally as beautiful a principle as mercy. Let me raise some questions: Who suffers most—the incest or rape victim; the physically abused spouse; the paraplegic; those with debilitating diseases; those who lose a child, a parent, or a spouse; those who are unemployed; those who suffer as manic depressed, or the liar, the thief; or those involved in abortions, homosexuality, and similar unnatural sins? Who suffers most— the adulterer or the parents who have a wayward son or daughter? I believe the parents who have a wayward child suffer at least as much if not more than an adulterer. Such heartfelt suffering is expressed in this beautiful verse:

WHERE IS MY WANDERING BOY TONIGHT?

Where is my wandering boy tonight?
　　the boy of my tend'rest care:
The boy that was once my joy and light, the child of my
　　love and prayer.

Once he was pure as the morning dew, as he knelt at his
　　mother's knee;
No face was so bright, no heart more true, and none was as
　　sweet as he.

Oh, could I see him now, my boy, as fair as in olden time,
When prattle and smile made home a joy, and life was a
　　merry chime.
Go, for my wandering boy tonight, go search for him where
　　you will:

But bring him to me with all his blight, and tell him I love
    him still.

Oh, where is my boy tonight? where is my boy tonight?
My heart o'erflows, for I love him, he knows,
Oh, where is my boy tonight?

(ANONYMOUS.)

The adulterer can meet with a common judge, and, when
repentance is complete, that priesthood leader can forgive the sin
on behalf of the Church. Parents of a wayward one have a void and
a heartache that will not go away until the straying one returns.
The parents are innocent. Does justice somehow demand that they
should suffer so deeply? Is it just for children to be born on a
garbage dump in the Philippines, Rwanda, or even the United
States, or in diseased and poverty-stricken communities in
Mexico, South America, or anywhere else in the world? Is it just for
other children to be born in homes where God knows they will be
abused through incest or brutality—tortured and maimed by evil
parents? Is it just for women, youth, and children to be abused or
raped in their innocence without penalty to the offender? My
answer is an unmistakable *no!*

In God's great goodness He has provided justice. Some years
ago I was invited to speak at the funeral service for Rachael
Runyan, a beautiful, blonde-haired, blue-eyed girl. I believe she
was three or four years old. She had been kidnapped, and the
entire nation was incensed at this act of horror as they sympa-
thized with the anguished parents. Weeks later her body was found
partially buried on a creek bank. She had been violated and must
have been terrified beyond anything we can imagine for one so
innocent and young.

I read and studied to prepare a funeral sermon, but I could
not find anything that I thought could bring comfort to the parents, who must have trembled at thoughts of the horrific indigni-
ties suffered by this sweet little innocent soul. The day of the
funeral I went to my office early and knelt in solitude. I pled with

the Lord that I might be able to say something that would bring peace to two wonderful, innocent parents who had suffered more than anyone ought to suffer. Then I sat at my desk and began to write. The pen raced across the page sentence after sentence.

In essence, I explained at the funeral that as soon as that sweet, little soul had passed through the veil, she would have been cradled in the arms of a loving Father in Heaven. With one caress He could remove every horror, every terror, every indignity as though it had never happened. I then explained that if God could do that on the other side of the veil, I was convinced that He could do the same on this side of the veil for Rachael's parents. They could know that their innocent, sweet little daughter was totally healed. They need not carry the burden of hate, vengeance, anger, and bitterness that cankers and darkens the soul. According to the supreme goodness of God, they could leave justice to Him. Justice is beautiful and will be satisfied. Nothing shall be left undone.

I thank God every day of my life for other dimensions of the Atonement. Christ not only ransomed us from our sins, but also He suffered for the "pains and afflictions and temptations of every kind; and this that the word might be fulfilled which saith he will take upon him the pains and the sicknesses of his people." (Alma 7:11.) It would only be just that the innocent find comfort, relief, and peace through Jesus as the transgressors do. If He can carry the burden of our transgressions, it would only be just that the innocent have their pain and afflictions removed as well.

Every victim of incest, rape, spouse abuse, molestation, and fraud is equally entitled to relief and peace and should be as free from suffering as the repentant transgressor. If the transgressor alone could find peace and forgiveness, where would be the justice? The Redeemer of the world has redeemed the innocent and has atoned for the suffering of the innocent as well as the guilty. All souls who suffer are invited to come unto Him. "Come unto me," He entreated, "all ye that labour and are heavy laden, and I will give you rest. Take my yoke upon you, and learn of me; for I am meek and lowly in heart: and ye shall find rest unto your souls.

For my yoke is easy, and my burden is light." (Matthew 11:28–30.) He who has borne all burdens has asked that we transfer the horror and terror, the scars of suffering, the baggage we have carried for so many years to Him. This transfer takes place in the same way for the victim as it does for the transgressor. Alma cried, "O Jesus, thou Son of God, have mercy on me, who am in the gall of bitterness, and am encircled about by the everlasting chains of death. And now, behold, when I thought this, I could remember my pains no more; yea, I was harrowed up by the memory of my sins no more. And oh, what joy, and what marvelous light I did behold." (Alma 36:18–20.) His soul was filled with joy exquisite and sweet.

King Lamoni's father cried out, "O God, Aaron hath told me that there is a God; and if there is a God, and if thou art God, wilt thou make thyself known unto me, and I will give away all my sins to know thee." (Alma 22:18.)

When we really believe that Christ will take upon Himself our afflictions, our illnesses and sicknesses, we will do what Alma and King Lamoni's father did. We will go to Him who can take the weight of our trials and sufferings from us. The Master in His loving goodness will surely bring relief to the innocent victims of horrible deeds as to those who transgress. That is true justice.

Justice demands that there be compensating blessings for every particle of suffering we go through innocently. When a child or adult is sexually or physically abused, he or she should feel no guilt or loss of virtue or chastity. A person may be violated, but it is my faith that virginity and chastity in the eyes of God cannot be taken from innocent victims. A person who is robbed financially or materially does not need to see the bishop to see if any action should be taken against him. He is an innocent victim. The same thing is true of incest and rape victims. They are innocent before God, and I witness that a loving Savior can remove every heartache, terror, horror, feeling of shame, or loss of esteem. He can fill the soul with joy, marvelous light, and exquisite sweetness. If He did that only for the sinful, He would not be just. But He is a merciful God, and He has done it for the innocent and the repentant alike.

We must not add to the burdens carried by the innocent victim. When the future conduct of a violated one is warped and veers away from normal Christian conduct because of the abuse he or she has suffered, I believe that the Lord will be extremely merciful. I am persuaded that the Lord will judge them for what they would have been had the abuse never occurred.

No man should ever physically abuse his wife or any other woman. B. H. Roberts said, "Men who are fiercest with men are gentlest with women." (Truman Madsen, *Defender of the Faith*, p. 96.) Any who are caught up in the vicious sin of abusing others, who will not follow counsel but continue their abusive ways, are not worthy of full fellowship in the God of Mercy's kingdom. Jacob said, "And I will not suffer, saith the Lord of Hosts, that the cries of the fair daughters of this people . . . shall come up unto me against the men of my people. . . . For they shall not lead away captive the daughters of my people because of their tenderness, save I shall visit them with a sore curse, even unto destruction." (Jacob 2:32–33.)

What brought on this harsh warning? "I, the Lord, have seen the sorrow, and heard the mourning of the daughters of my people . . . because of the wickedness and abominations of their husbands. . . . Ye have broken the hearts of your tender wives, and lost the confidence of your children, because of your bad examples . . . [and] many hearts died, pierced with deep wounds." (Jacob 2:31, 35.)

The demands of justice require that those who commit such horrible acts against children, wives—indeed against any child of God—not go unnoticed and unpunished. Justice demands full and complete restitution, either through repentance or personal suffering. The Savior said, "I command you to repent—repent, lest I smite you by the rod of my mouth, and by my wrath, and by my anger, and your sufferings be sore—how sore you know not, how exquisite you know not, yea, how hard to bear you know not. For behold, I, God, have suffered these things for all, that they might not suffer if they would repent; But if they would not repent they must suffer even as I; Which suffering caused myself, even God, the greatest of all, to tremble because of pain, and to bleed at every pore, and to suffer both body and spirit." (D&C 19:15–18.)

It would only be just that perpetrators of incest, rape, and spouse abuse be held accountable; if they repent not, they must suffer, though "how exquisite" that suffering will be they know not!

The innocent victim should not be required to carry guilt and scars and baggage of shame. A loving and willing Master desires to lift those things from our hearts and minds and replace them with His love and sweet peace. Christ will take on Himself our illnesses, our sicknesses, our sufferings—but we must let Him. Only in this way will the demands of justice be met not only for the very, very wicked who do such foul deeds but also for the wonderfully sweet, innocent victims.

Those who do not transfer to Jesus their sorrows and heartache—those who want revenge, who have bitterness and hate for those who have offended and violated them—carry a weight too burdensome to carry alone.

Do not put time limits on justice against the wicked. Many men and women leave this life without ever having felt a particle of guilt, some without having had their vile crimes detected. They have felt no remorse for their conduct. They may even have served in Church callings and had wonderful reputations, wealth, good health, and glowing funeral services. Do not be concerned; the demands of justice reach beyond the veil! The important thing is for those who are innocent victims to remember the words of the Lord: "Be still and know that I am God." (D&C 110:16.) We must forgive and leave judgment to Him who promised justice. President Harold B. Lee said, after he had been called as an apostle, "I came to a night some years ago, when on my bed, I realized that before I could be worthy of the high place to which I had been called, I must love and forgive every soul that walked the earth, and in that time I came to know and I received a peace and a direction, and a comfort and an inspiration, that told me things to come and gave me impressions that I knew were from a divine source." (Conference Report, October 1946, p. 46.) We also must forgive and leave justice to God.

Our daughter has four sons. This last summer we were at Philmont together. The oldest son, Joshua, was six; Christian, not yet five; Michael, two; and the new baby but two months old. Joshua, as the oldest, had been given certain responsibilities and was a little older, so he had an established position of authority. Michael, two, was hardly old enough to be concerned about a new baby; besides, Michael was at that wonderfully fun, perpetually happy age. The baby, of course, was often the focus of much of the family affection. Christian, almost five, could see all the attention that Michael and the baby were getting; he must have felt neglected and needed to know his place and whether he was loved.

I was in the living room of the cottage provided for us when Christian's need bubbled out. My wife, Merlene, and Christian were in the kitchen. I heard this little boy say to his grandmother, "Grandma, do you like me?" Then I heard coming from the other room, "Oh, Christian, I love you with all my heart and soul." In a few minutes, Christian came out of the kitchen, a sweet smile glowing on his face.

Years ago, Joe J. Christensen quoted Urie Bronfenbrenner, who said, "It's good for a child to be in the company of people who are crazy about him for a substantial number of hours every day." (*Psychology Today,* March 1977, p. 43.)

As children of God, we have a Father in Heaven who has an unlimited, unconditional love for each one of us, and I believe if we listen carefully, we can hear Him say, "I love you with all my heart and soul." I promise in His holy name that He will extend mercy. He will be just, for justice cannot be destroyed. Justice is a dimension of charity, the pure love of Christ. I love and thank God for His mercy and for His justice.

CHAPTER THREE

· · ·

# The Master, the Winepress, and Us

At a stake conference in Cebu in the Philippines, I met an unusual pair. The Huguettes were middle-aged—a brother and a sister. The woman was waiting for her brother just outside the door of the men's restroom. In a moment he called to her. She went inside and bent down; he, holding onto a divider for support, climbed onto her back. She then carried him into the chapel for our priesthood meeting. When the meeting was over, Brother Huguette's sister was not close by, so I volunteered to carry him where he needed to go. He was not light—I would estimate he weighed 150 pounds or more. They lived over a kilometer from the chapel. I understood that there were times when she carried him all the way to church. Other times she carried him to a place where they could catch a jeepney and ride to church.

You may recall having read about them in the *Church News.* Later the *Church Almanac* used a picture of the couple on the inside of the back cover. We all remember the beautiful saying, "He's not heavy, he's my brother." It would be interesting and humbling if somehow we could determine the total number of kilometers and the total number of times Sister Huguette has carried her brother on her back.

The Huguettes are just two of all the myriad souls who walk the earth. We would be staggered to know the totality of this wonderful woman's commitment to serve her brother. Over the years she has had little or no help. Sister Huguette exemplifies well the fact that in life, some of our Saints "tread their own private wine-press alone."

In order to comprehend the Master's love, we must go to the scriptures and mine the riches they contain. We need to understand how the Atonement works in our behalf, not only for our sins but also for the suffering that comes to us in so many other ways.

Nephi was permitted a special and spiritual experience as he beheld the Spirit of God. The Spirit of God questioned him, "Knowest thou the condescension of God?" (1 Nephi 11:16.) Nephi responded, "I know that he loveth his children; nevertheless, I do not know the meaning of all things." (Verse 17.) Nephi beheld the virgin Mary and saw that she was carried away in the Spirit. "And after she had been carried away in the Spirit for the space of a time the angel spake unto me, saying: Look!" (Verse 19.) As he looked he beheld the virgin again, bearing a child in her arms.

"And the angel said unto me: Behold the Lamb of God, yea, even the Son of the Eternal Father!" (Verse 21.) It was this Only Begotten Son of the God of heaven who would exclaim, "I have overcome and have trodden the wine-press alone, even the wine-press of the fierceness of the wrath of Almighty God." (D&C 76:107.) He essentially makes the same lonely statement again in section 133 of the Doctrine and Covenants, commencing with verse 50: "I have trodden the wine-press alone, and have brought judgment upon all people; and none were with me." I feel a certain sense of loneliness—and perhaps hurt—whenever I read His words. He then goes on to say: "And I have trampled them in my fury, and I did tread upon them in mine anger, and their blood have I sprinkled upon my garments, and stained all my raiment; for this was the day of vengeance which was in my heart." (D&C 133:51.)

The more pure in heart we are, the more we despise sin. The Master, in an incomprehensible way, saw and felt the most dastardly of acts that can be perpetrated by one person on another. Acts such as murder, abortion, incest, pedophilia, homosexuality, adultery, fornication, and brutality might well have prompted the fury and anger with which He uttered the above warning.

In dramatic contrast, the Lord then says: "And now the year of my redeemed is come; and they shall mention the loving kindness of their Lord, and all that he has bestowed upon them according to his goodness, and according to his loving kindness, forever and ever. In all their afflictions he was afflicted. And the angel of his presence saved them; and in his love, and in his pity, he redeemed them, and bore them." (D&C 133:52–53.)

One morning our executive secretary in the Philippines came into my office. He said, "Look over at the temple." I looked across the street and saw a woman walking on her knees, dragging her crippled legs behind her. A woman walked on either side of her; each one held one of her hands. They walked with her as they would with a child. (She must have had incredibly calloused knees. In the Philippines sidewalks are often made from crushed gravel so that they will not be slick when it rains. Most of us could not have walked but a few steps on our knees before they would have been torn and bloody.)

I called downstairs to our welfare department and asked them how long it would take them to buy a wheelchair. They thought they could get one in an hour or so. We gave approval, and one of our bishops went out and bought a wheelchair. He took it to the temple, hid it behind a pillar, and waited. In a few minutes this sweet little soul came out of the temple, walking on her knees with her two friends on either side. The bishop stopped the woman and asked, "Do you have a wheelchair?" She responded, "I used to, but it was old and fell apart and was beyond repair." It is doubtful that this sister ever again could have saved up enough money to buy a wheelchair. The bishop asked her if she would like a new one. She began to cry. Both ladies who were with her became emotional. The bishop reached behind the pillar and pulled out the new wheelchair. It was a humbly tender moment for all involved.

A short time after that, that same bishop, Bishop Santos, was in my office again. He had a form requesting a substantial amount of money from our fast-offering funds. A boy from a less-active family had a brain tumor and would die if it was not removed. As I recollect, the surgery had to be done in Manila. The bishop had requested financial assistance. He said, "Elder Featherstone, I know we cannot afford to send that much money out of our ward's fast offerings. We have checked with the charity hospital, and the boy would be on a waiting list for at least a year." Bishop Santos said, "I am here for counsel. What do we do for this little boy?" I pondered for a moment and then felt impressed to say, "Bishop, give me the form. I will approve the request." When I looked up from signing the request form, Bishop Santos was weeping. He said, "Elder Featherstone, we belong to a magnificent and wonderful church." I replied, "We do, bishop, we really do." Many members of the Church unknowingly joined together to extend to a young boy mercy and life.

Through such acts, we begin to have some small understanding of justice and mercy. To the unrepentant sinner will come anger, justice, and suffering. In Doctrine and Covenants 19:4, the Lord declared there are only two courses open to us: "And surely every man must repent or suffer." There is no third option. The Lord further stated: "Wherefore, I revoke not the judgments which I shall pass, but woes shall go forth, weeping, wailing and gnashing of teeth, yea, to those who are found on my left hand." (D&C 19:5.) Those who choose not to repent are on the left hand.

However, because of his love for us, Christ vicariously suffered for all who would repent. So exquisite, so bitter, so hard to bear was the suffering even for Him, that He in great mercy powerfully declared: "Therefore I command you to repent—repent, lest I smite you by the rod of my mouth, and by my wrath, and by my anger, and your sufferings be sore—how sore you know not, how exquisite you know not, yea, how hard to bear you know not. For behold, I, God, have suffered these things for all, that they might not suffer if they would repent." (D&C 19:15–16.)

It would be difficult for a man who has lost his wife or a child to explain his heartsick soul suffering to one who has never experienced such grief. Well might this man say, "I pray to God that you never have to experience what I have been through." The Savior, I believe, was letting us know that none of us ever would want to go through what He suffered in Gethsemane.

Where there are laws, they must be obeyed. If they are not obeyed, there must be a punishment. If they are obeyed, there is a blessing. But who metes out the punishment? "For, behold, the mystery of godliness, how great is it! For, behold, I am endless, and the punishment which is given from my hand is endless punishment, for Endless is my name. Wherefore—Eternal punishment is God's punishment. Endless punishment is God's punishment." (D&C 19:10–12.)

This does not presuppose that the punishment from God is without end or eternal in nature. As clarified by the Lord, Eternal or Endless are other titles for Him. He might have said "Jehovah's punishment." It would have meant the same as Eternal or Endless punishment.

Why would God say, "Repent, lest I smite you by the rod of my mouth and by my wrath, and by my anger, and your sufferings be sore"? To some degree, Alma the Younger helped us to understand this as he bore his testimony to his son Helaman: "So great had been my iniquities, that the very thought of coming into the presence of my God did rack my soul with inexpressible horror. Oh, thought I, that I could be banished and become extinct both soul and body, that I might not be brought to stand in the presence of my God, to be judged of my deeds. And now, for three days and for three nights was I racked, even with the pains of a damned soul." Later he added: "Yea, I say unto you, my son, that there could be nothing so exquisite and so bitter as were my pains." (Alma 36:14–16, 21.)

Those who choose not to repent, who take pleasure in their sins of incest, child abuse, homosexuality, abortion, adultery, and similar abominations, will feel the wrath of the Law Enforcer, whose name is Eternal and Endless. He will smite them by the rod of His mouth. How is this done?

"All spirit is matter, but it is more fine or pure." (D&C 131:7.) Furthermore, "the word of the Lord is truth, and whatsoever is truth is light, and whatsoever is light is Spirit, even the Spirit of Jesus Christ." (D&C 84:45.) If spirit is matter, and if light is Spirit, and truth is light, then how powerful is truth? Could truth be tangible? Could the Lawgiver enforce the laws of His everlasting gospel with truth? Is it not so, surely, that the truth from "the rod of His mouth" will provide the punishment? (D&C 19:15.)

Alma had been confronted by the angel for his sin and was told: "Seek no more to destroy the church of God." (Alma 36:9.) Nowhere does it state that he was involved in sexual transgressions or murder, yet we sometimes hear speakers interpreting his words in that way. He actually said, "I had murdered many of his children," then he corrected himself and said, "Rather led them away unto destruction." (Verse 14.) His exquisite suffering for three days and nights, he described in these words: "Racked with torment, . . . I was harrowed up by the memory [truth] of my many sins . . . in the gall of bitterness, encircled about by the everlasting chains of death." (Verses 17–18.) We do not understand how powerful truth is—either its saving effect on the righteous or its absolute accusative spirit against the wicked. I wonder if truth does not pervade every fiber and cell of the body, even to the marrow of the bones. To the righteous and repentant, it is glorious beyond all that words can say. To the wicked it will be terrible and penetrating, as much as the physical body and the mind can endure, and perhaps more.

Imagine the rod of the mouth of God punishing in His wrath those who commit incest or similar evils. How is it possible to comprehend the suffering through which the unrepentant will go? Their punishment will be Endless (God's) punishment. Those who have chosen not to repent will suffer until they have paid the full demands of justice. Once justice has been satisfied through their own personal suffering, then their debt will have been paid in full. But let there be no doubt—they will either repent or suffer.

The Atonement was also wrought on behalf of the illnesses, sicknesses, and afflictions of the world. "In all their afflictions he was afflicted." (D&C 133:53.) Indeed, Matthew recorded that the Master "Himself took our infirmities, and bare our sicknesses." (Matthew 8:17.) Alma teaches this same truth: "And he shall go forth, suffering pains and afflictions and temptations of every kind; and this that the word might be fulfilled which saith he will take upon him the pains and the sicknesses of his people. And he will take upon him death, that he may loose the bands of death which bind his people; and he will take upon him their infirmities, that his bowels may be filled with mercy, according to the flesh, that he may know according to the flesh how to succor his people according to their infirmities." (Alma 7:11–12.)

What a magnificent concept: Christ did take on *all* our suffering so "that he may know according to the flesh how to succor his people." To succor suggests "to relieve, benefit, avail, be of some good help, befriend, lend or bear a hand, be the making of, or to see one through." Succor is what those who understand and practice charity do. To succor means that we are fulfilling a dimension of charity. Charity is the pure love of Christ, a love that never fails. When we succor, we come near the Savior-like attitude of mercy. We do what the Master Himself would do, and we do what He would have us do.

How do the Atonement and the Redemption blend to bring about the grand blessing of having the Savior promise to succor those who are in need? It is my feeling that part of the Atonement was wrought for all the righteous and worthy, the honorable and needy both in and out of the Church. Consider, as we must so often, the destructive results of divorce, child abuse, and family abandonment on the innocent. Why do the innocent suffer? Because God will not take away our agency. Therefore, those who choose to violate the commandments always leave a "trail of tears" in the lives of the innocent. The innocent should not have to suffer for another's transgression any more than all mankind should suffer for Adam's sin. However, all trials we go through in life are a testing. The innocent are not spared. Sometimes even the most perfect suffer more than the most wicked. The Savior is the supernal example. More recently, we have seen President Spencer W. Kimball—an apostle, holy and pure, filled with love—endure some of the greatest of trials.

Consider the lesson taught by the following true story. A young man was converted to the Church. His father died when this young man was but a boy. Before he died, the father gave his only possession of any value to his wife to give to his son when he grew up—a ring with a beautiful stone in it. The mother kept the ring until the boy was in high school; then she gave it to him. When he graduated from high school, his mother bought him a fine watch. It was all this woman could afford.

When her son joined the Church, she was offended and became critical. Their relationship became greatly strained. The young man's bishop interviewed him, and shortly thereafter he was called on a mission. When he told his mother, she was irate. She said she would not give him one penny of support. When he left home to travel to Manila to the Missionary Training Center, he had no money. He took a taxi from the airport to the MTC. He had no money to pay. He offered his watch as payment, and the driver gladly took it. Because he knew he had no money to cover costs at the MTC, he went to a pawnshop, pawned his ring, and then reported at the MTC.

At a zone conference some months later, this wonderful young elder recounted how he had financed his way to the MTC. Then he said with great emotion, "I don't have my graduation watch my mother gave me, and I sold the ring my dad gave me, but I am serving my Savior on a mission, and it is worth it." Our faith is tried in many different ways, but I believe the most difficult trials come when we have to choose between the Savior and His work and our family.

In the following poem, Ella Wheeler Wilcox teaches us that we all will face our "Gethsemanes."

### GETHSEMANE

In golden youth when seems the earth
A Summer-land of singing mirth,
When souls are glad and hearts are light,
And not a shadow lurks in sight,
We do not know it, but there lies
Somewhere veiled under evening skies
A garden which we all must see—
The garden of Gethsemane.

With joyous steps we go our ways,
Love lends a halo to our days;
Light sorrows sail like clouds afar,
We laugh, and say how strong we are.
We hurry on; and hurrying, go
Close to the border-land of woe,
That waits for you, and waits for me—
For ever waits Gethsemane.

Down shadowy lanes, across strange streams,
Bridged over by our broken dreams;
Behind the misty caps of years,
Beyond the great salt fount of tears,
The garden lies. Strive as you may,
You cannot miss it in your way.
All paths that have been, or shall be,
Pass somewhere through Gethsemane.

All those who journey, soon or late,
Must pass within the garden's gate;

Must kneel alone in darkness there,
And battle with some fierce despair.
God pity those who cannot say,
"Not mine but thine," who only pray,
"Let this cup pass," and cannot see
The *purpose* in Gethsemane.

(*POEMS OF POWER* [CHICAGO:
W. B. CONKEY CO.], PP. 147–48.)

I do not doubt but what it might be more difficult to keep our second estate than our first. However, when we understand the eternal purpose of pain, trials, testings, and unjust criticism, our souls begin to expand. We develop glorious, tender traits of kindness, thoughtfulness, and understanding. We more easily empathize with others who suffer as we have done. We realize how fragile life can be. We learn to understand the delicate balance that weighs sometimes for, sometimes against, us.

The Lord gave His children resiliency. Job loved and honored God as few men ever have. Even when he seemed to lose hope in ever again finding peace in this life, he never lost his faith in God. His mental anguish at the loss of all of his sons and daughters after the wind caused the house to collapse must have been almost as much as mortals can bear. His loss of earthly wealth would have staggered the most solid. Afflictions came in the form of boils, yet he uttered not one negative word against his God. So great was his faith that, millennia later when the Prophet Joseph would cry out from Liberty Jail, "Oh, God, where art thou?" the Lord told Joseph, "Thou art not yet as Job; thy friends do not contend against thee, neither charge thee with transgression, as they did Job." (D&C 121:10.)

When we ponder Job's affliction, we must consider the loss of his family, his herds and flocks, and his health. When the Savior comforted Joseph Smith, He focused on Job's friends abandoning him and accusing him falsely of transgression. Is there a message for us to learn here? I think so. Perhaps this lesson hearkens back to His statement, "I have trodden the wine-press alone." (D&C 133:5.) No one could have helped Him or could even begin to understand the total abandonment and loneliness that the Atonement would bring.

I believe that Jesus knew that physical pain and financial reverses were temporary but that false accusations and having friends turn against us were lifelong maladies from which few would escape. He reminded those who would follow Him, "Judge not that ye be not judged." (Matthew 7:1.) We do not know the smallest part of the Atonement's full effects.

The widow or widower, the orphan, the divorced person—all suffer excruciatingly. There is comfort to know that He has suffered for the afflictions and illnesses of the world. He reminds us of this part of His ministry in these words: "Listen to him who is the advocate with the Father, who is pleading your cause before him—Saying: Father, behold the sufferings and death of him who did no sin, in whom thou wast well pleased; behold the blood of thy Son which was shed, the blood of him whom thou gavest that thyself might be glorified." (D&C 45:3–4.)

An advocate is an intercessor. The great intercessory prayer, as recorded in John 17, provides a profound example: "These words spake Jesus, and lifted up his eyes to heaven." (Verse 1.) Eyes lifted heavenward often show equally as great humility as those closed with bowed head. In this position He humbly pled, "Father, the hour is come; glorify thy Son, that thy Son also may glorify thee." (Verse 1.) What a great lesson in humility and meekness! When we receive glory—that is, attention and honor—in our callings or for a given performance, should we not desire the glory only insofar as it glorifies our Lord or His Church?

Christ's divine prayer continued: "As thou hast given him power over all flesh, that he should give eternal life to as many as thou hast given him." (Verse 2.) Baptism ties directly to the Atonement. When we have received baptism, we are His. We partake of the sacrament, the ordinance which ties most directly to the Atonement, to renew our covenants and to acknowledge by our own volition that we are His and will live in accordance to His commandments.

Then He gives us the great key to eternal life: "And this is life eternal, that they might know thee the only true God, and Jesus Christ, whom thou hast sent." (Verse 3.) He refers to Himself in His God-ordained role as the Christ. Knowing God is more than just having read about His life or even having lived His commandments and served faithfully in the Church. All these things are essential, but to really know a person is greater than even those things. We know that each member of the Godhead knows us. There is no façade for them; no inner thought not perceived; no motivation, doubt, fear, faith, love; no act—however pure or vile— nothing we have ever done in our lifetime that is not known to Them. We all stand as transparent crystal before Them, and They see our innermost recesses.

When we come to know the Master as a friend and we comprehend His stature in the eternities; when we understand the Atonement, His condescensions, His love, His sacrifice and spotless life; when we clearly perceive that all this has been given for the benefit of mankind—when we come to this point, then we begin to know Him. The Nephites with whom He spent a significant period of time looked "upon him as if they would ask him to tarry a little longer with them." (3 Nephi 17:5.) One who truly knows Him does not—nor cannot, nor will not—forget Him, ever. Whatever daily task, pleasure, sport, or activity we may be involved in, His desires are supreme in our lives. If we become careless in the way we wear the garment, haphazardly use the Lord's name, or serve only socially in the Church, we clearly do not "know" the Master. We might even know the Church is true, but actually knowing Jesus Christ would dramatically change our conduct. We would no longer have a disposition to do evil; rather, we would feel absolutely submissive to His will and turn our lives over to Him. Knowing Him is much, much more than knowing about Him. And eternal life is to know Him and His Father. A cross-reference to this verse leads us back to John 10, where the Savior teaches, "My sheep hear my voice, and I know them, and they follow me." (Verse 27.) That is the answer: to know Him is to follow Him. He continues, "I give unto them eternal life; and they shall never perish, neither shall any man pluck them out of my hand." (Verse 28.)

In the fourth verse of John 17, Jesus declared, "I have finished the work which thou gavest me to do." He had put a cause in motion that could not change course; Gethsemane and Calvary still lay ahead, but the work was finished.

And so He continued with His great intercessory prayer: "I have manifested thy name unto the men which thou gavest me out of the world: thine they were, and thou gavest them me; and they have kept thy word. Now they have known that all things whatsoever thou hast given me are of thee . . . and they have believed that thou didst send me. . . . I pray for them . . . for they are thine. And now come I to thee; and these things I speak in the world, that they might have my joy fulfilled in themselves." (John 17:6–9, 13.)

This is an interesting consideration on the Master's part. What does it mean to have his "joy fulfilled in themselves"? Could it possibly mean the joy we feel as a convert comes into the Church, a wayward son or daughter returns home, or a family we have taught is sealed at the altar in the temple? Could He mean that we see our children serve and love Him or feel the joy of caring for the widow, the orphan, the poor, the sick, and all others who touch our lives? I am persuaded that there is no joy in this life comparable to the joy of the Lord.

Later, in verses 16 and 17, we read: "They are not of the world, even as I am not of the world. Sanctify them through thy truth: thy word is truth."

Remember our earlier discussion on truth. Sanctification means to be made pure and spotless and holy. Truth can sanctify us if we abide in it. Truth purges falsehoods, misconceptions, errors, lies, evil, lusting, and other perverse behaviors from our lives. Truth is greater than the sword. Jesus' prayer to His Father included the admission that "thy word is truth." All truth emanates from God. Truth is eternal and absolute, and it sanctifies those who receive it.

Verse 19 states: "And for their sakes I sanctify myself, that they also might be sanctified through the truth." The footnote attached to the word *sanctify* in this verse refers the reader to the Topical Guide entry entitled "Jesus Christ, Atonement through." Most of us who have faith in Christ go through a sanctification when we suffer physically or mentally.

Note how the intercessory prayer anticipates the Atonement and Christ's suffering in Gethsemane.

The Atonement and sanctification wrap themselves around the believer. Christ prayed: "Neither pray I for these alone, but for them also which shall believe on me through their word; that they all may be one; as thou, Father, art in me, and I in thee, that they also may be one in us." (Verse 20.) And then the Master explains the great purpose in this unity: "That the world may believe that thou hast sent me." (Verse 20.)

This great truth about unity was of such consequence that it was one of the major things for which Christ prayed in His intercessory prayer. We do not yet comprehend the power and the spiritual strength that will come to the Church when we are totally united in truth and have become sanctified. A power surge would come from this Church that would startle the world and reach into every nation, state, community, village, and home, as it did in the days of Enoch and as it will yet happen during the millennial reign.

The Savior concludes His great prayer with these words: "O righteous Father, the world hath not known thee: but I have known thee and these have known that thou hast sent me. And I have declared unto them thy name, and will declare it: that the love wherewith thou hast loved me may be in them, and I in them." (Verses 25–26.)

As we read the intercessory prayer, we receive some small understanding of what it means to "know thee, the only true God, and Jesus Christ, whom thou hast sent." (Verse 3.)

The apostles who knelt with Christ at the Last Supper had the glorious opportunity of having God the Son, the Redeemer, pray for them. Can we conceive of this magnificent experience? As recorded in 3 Nephi, two thousand five hundred souls exclaimed: "And no tongue can speak, neither can there be written by any man, neither can the hearts of men conceive so great and marvelous things as we both saw and heard Jesus speak; and no one can conceive of the joy which filled our souls at the time we heard him pray for us unto the Father. And it came to pass that when Jesus had made an end of praying unto the Father, he arose; but so great was the joy of the multitude that they were overcome." (3 Nephi 17: 17–18.)

Joy, truth, sanctification, unity, salvation, and exaltation are all tied to the Atonement. Justice and mercy are fulfilled because He, the Master of heaven and earth, the Only Begotten, trod the winepress alone. Of all who walked the earth, He alone qualified to satisfy the eternal demands of justice. We—all of humanity—stood by helplessly as He alone faced that most excruciating trial. Many of us would have given our lives to have accompanied Him through that agonizing hour, but, alas, not one other was qualified. We praise His name forever and forever—and pray that we will be worthy to know Him.

## CHAPTER FOUR

# Who Is This Jesus?

A few years ago, I was in Canada at a "Nathan Eldon Tanner" camp. This experience paralleled the Boy Scout training that we provide at Philmont, except that we took the training to the good Saints of Canada instead of having them travel all the way to New Mexico. We even brought with us our own instructors and youth leaders.

During that week the staff organized a "Polar Bear" club. In order to qualify, a person had to swim at six o'clock four mornings in a row in the cold Elbow River. It had just snowed eight inches at an elevation just one thousand feet higher than our camp. The first morning I went down to the river with the group. I have always had a difficult time wading into a lake or river slowly. I would rather have one giant, breathtaking shock than the dozens of painful ones that come from slowly wading into the river. I filled my lungs with all the air they could hold so I could not suck in anything else when the shock of the cold water caused me to catch my breath, then dived in—it was ice cold! Without wasting any time, I swam out to the middle of the river, where the water was almost chest deep.

In a moment a stake president dove in and swam up right beside me. After the shock of the cold wore off a bit, he said, "Did I have my glasses on?" I replied, "I don't know, did you?" He said he thought he had, so I told him I thought he should swim back to the bank and see. In a moment he came back and replied, "I did have them on." The Elbow River was flowing about ten to twelve miles an hour, I estimated. I was sure that his glasses were now on their way down the river toward Calgary.

My heart went out to him. Here was a stake president who had spent hundreds of dollars to drive from western Canada to Calgary, bringing his whole family in an older, wood-paneled station wagon, as I recall. He had all the expenses of gasoline, lodging, and meals coming, as well as the training fees. I knew the camp must have been a terrific financial strain on him. Certainly he could not afford $200 or $300 for a new pair of glasses.

I walked upstream about thirty or forty feet. Offering a prayer, I asked God to help me find those glasses. Mind you, it was six o'clock in the morning; the water was cold and clear and flowing relatively fast. I lay down on my back and floated downstream. Suddenly I had an impression and stopped. When I stood up, I looked down at the water and thought I could see something glistening on the bottom of the river. Quickly I dove down and came up with the stake president's glasses.

Who is this Jesus who not only created the earth but also takes such a personal interest in His friends and servants that He would help find a pair of glasses for a stake president?

One day Elder Ted E. Brewerton and I were talking. He had made some calculations. He had determined that a million seconds is twelve days; a billion seconds is thirty-two years. This started me thinking about a talk I had given. Astronomers claim that we can see approximately 5,000 stars with the naked eye on a clear night with no moon. We can see 50,000 stars with a pair of binoculars. With a high-powered telescope we can see across our galaxy. We are on the outside edge of the Milky Way galaxy, which astronomers estimate has 600 billion stars and is hundreds of billions of miles across. On a clear night, we can see something of the pattern created by these billions of stars. But we are not alone: astronomers have discovered twenty-one additional galaxies.

The book of Moses states:

> And he [Moses] beheld also the inhabitants thereof, and there was not a soul which he beheld not; and he discerned them by the Spirit of God; and their numbers were great, even numberless as the sand upon the sea shore.
>
> And he beheld many lands; and each land was called earth, and there were inhabitants on the face thereof.
>
> And it came to pass that Moses called upon God, saying: Tell me, I pray thee, why these things are so, and by what thou madest them? (Moses 1:28–30.)

Later, in chapter 7 of Moses, verses 28–30, Enoch revealed the vastness and the numbers of the Lord's creations:

> And it came to pass that the God of heaven looked upon the residue of the people, and he wept; and Enoch bore record of it, saying: How is it that the heavens weep, and shed forth their tears as the rain upon the mountains?
>
> And Enoch said unto the Lord: How is it that thou canst weep, seeing thou art holy, and from all eternity to all eternity?
>
> And were it possible that man could number the particles of the earth, yea, millions of earths like this, it would not be a beginning to the number of thy creations; and thy curtains are stretched out still; and yet thou art there, and thy bosom is there; and also thou art just; thou art merciful and kind forever.

If we could "number the particles of the earth, yea millions of earths . . . it would not be a beginning to the number of thy creations." We have to surrender our puny understandings to an incomprehensible totality of creations by the Creator. Including every blade of grass, every flower, tree, shrub, animal, fish, insect, such a vision reaches far beyond our mortal ability to understand or comprehend.

And yet He touches our individual lives. At a recent zone conference, a young missionary stood and thanked me for blessing the missionaries and their parents, brothers, sisters, and other family members. He thanked the Lord for the blessing that his mother and other family members would not go hungry while he was on a mission. He was grateful for the blessing of protection on his loved ones. Then with great feeling, this wonderful young elder said, "My mother is a single parent. She works long hours to support two missionaries in the field." Then he told of having a sister also on a mission and explained that his mother faithfully sent money to the bishop every month to support her missionary children. I felt a rush of love and tenderness for that wonderful woman who was providing for a family at home, paying her tithing, and supporting two missionaries. I imagine it has been a long time since she has bought anything for herself. But she knows the Master and He knows her. He knows her heart and the extent of her faith.

The Master is able to enlist not only this wonderful woman who would sacrifice and give all that she had but also all of the hosts of the earth who call themselves Christians. Again we ask, "Who is this Jesus who causes us to do—and feel it a rare privilege—what no other power on the earth can do?"

The scientist in all his wisdom and intellectual capacity can make a seed that looks like a seed of grass. It is identical as far as the eye is concerned. You could not tell the real grass seed from the scientist-created one. Yet if you put both into the ground, only one would grow. In one is the seed of life, but not in the other.

Who is this Creator? It is my conviction that He who created worlds without number can also give power to His righteous, pure servants to heal the sick and bless the lives of people. Through His almighty power, the blind can and do see, the deaf hear, and the incurable become rid of hopeless disease.

This Jesus Christ whom we worship stands on the right hand of the Eternal God of the heavens and all earths. The supreme power in all that we comprehend and beyond is the great God of heaven, and Jesus is His Only Begotten Son.

How easily and simply some try to bring Him down to their level. Most Christians admit that Christ was a great prophet, the greatest teacher ever, the king of this world, and even the Savior. Few believe that He was literally, physically the Son of God. We do not understand the condescension of God, but we have the absolute witness that Jesus Christ is the Only Begotten of the Father. No member of this Church who studies the scriptures and understands the doctrine could ever think less.

What are God's limits? What are the bounds of His creations? What is the extent of His knowledge? What are the extremities of His compassion? Though some may attempt to place limits or bounds on Deity, what is that to God? No determination by mortals will ever change the absoluteness and totality of all that God is. We may not understand, but that is exactly what the problem is— we do not understand. That lack of understanding is by design, for thus we learn humility and faith. For now it is enough to know that there are absolute truths, and His perfection is absolute.

What are the capacities of Jesus Christ? We have the Light of Christ in our lives, as does every soul who ever has or does or will walk the earth.

Section 88 of the Doctrine and Covenants parts the veil for a small glimmer of the immortal Christ. Verse 6 describes Him as "He that ascended up on high." Begotten by God, our Heavenly Father, Creator of innumerable stars and planets, He is the second Being we worship in all of eternity. The verse goes on to state that "also he descended below all things." During the acts of the Atonement and the Crucifixion He suffered more than other mortals could bear: "How sore you know not, how exquisite you know not, yea, how hard to bear you know not." (D&C 19:15.) The combined weight of the transgression of the world and the full debt to satisfy justice were combined with the trials, diseases, and sicknesses of the world. No repentant sinner or innocent sufferer will ever be alone in that suffering. He has descended below all and knows every pang of sorrow, heartache, or remorse which we feel. The adulterer, homosexual, drug addict, thief, liar—all have the way opened to "turn from blotted archives of the past, and find the future's pages white as snow." ("Opportunity," in Ralph L. Woods, ed., *A Treasury of Inspiration* [New York: Thomas Y. Crowell Co., 1951], p. 83.) Thus He becomes our advocate with the Father:

> Listen to him who is the advocate with the Father, who is pleading your cause before him—
>
> Saying: Father, behold the sufferings and death of him who did no sin, in whom thou wast well pleased; behold the blood of thy Son which was shed, the blood of him whom thou gavest that thyself might be glorified;
>
> Wherefore, Father, spare these my brethren that believe on my name, that they may come unto me and have everlasting life. (D&C 45:3–5.)

We will not and cannot ever face a trial or sickness, transgression or trouble that He does not comprehend and understand. All these things He suffered vicariously; thus He became our advocate not only in repentance but also in trial.

Continuing verse 6 of Doctrine and Covenants 88, "Comprehended all things" means that He has perfect understanding in all things. Only in this way can He "be in all and through all things, the light of truth. Which truth shineth. This is the light of Christ." (D&C 88:6–7.) Doctrine and Covenants 84:45 helps us to understand that "the word of the Lord is truth, and whatsoever is truth is light, and whatsoever is light is Spirit, even the Spirit of Jesus Christ." Section 131, verse 7, states, "There is no such thing as immaterial matter. All spirit is matter, but it is more fine or pure."

"Also he is in the sun, and the light of the sun, and the power thereof by which it was made." (D&C 88:7.) The sun is 93 million miles from the earth. Imagine the energy that the sun perpetually produces. It takes the light from the sun a little less than eight and a half minutes to get to the earth. What power there is in the sun no mortal can possibly comprehend. Christ's power is not only in the light of the sun—it is also the power by which it was made. What knowledge must one have to create a sphere as large as the sun and put power into it, not for an hour or a day or one giant explosion, but for time unknown. What creative abilities did this Jesus have who could control the energy of the sun so it would be consistent from day to day, year to year, even millennium to millennium and beyond. As President Harold B. Lee stated, "The sun ripens the smallest bunch of grapes as though it had nothing else to do." We honor and glorify inventors of laser instruments, spacecrafts, heat-seeking missiles, atomic power facilities, television, and a multitude of other inventions. What are they compared to the sun, the earth, the moon, and the stars?

Verse 8 (D&C 88) states, "He is in the moon, and is the light of the moon, and the power thereof by which it was made." In verse 9 He is described as "the light of the stars, and the power thereof by which they were made." This statement is one about which we can only stand in total awe. What power is in this Jesus Christ that He created all these and remains as the power that governs their every movement?

"And the light which shineth, which giveth you light, is through him who enlighteneth your eyes, which is the same light that quickeneth your understandings; which light proceedeth forth from the presence of God to fill the immensity of space." (Verses 11–12.) Truth is light. Truth and light fill the immensity of space. Man in his puny effort cannot comprehend the smallest part of the power and glory and wisdom and knowledge of God. The prophets who have increased understanding cannot describe adequately the wonders of our God, this Jesus whom we worship.

What powers belonged to the premortal Jehovah as He stood as the Morning Star, the Day Star, and the Evening Star? What glorious powers did He receive as the Only Begotten of the Father? As the God of the Israelites and the whole of the Old Testament, what powers were His? What power would it take to part the waters of the Red Sea in an instant? Man in all his wisdom cannot do what to Christ is elementary, even rudimentary. Who among us can cause the earth or sun to not rotate so that there is a day and a night and a day without darkness? Who could save three Hebrew lads from a burning, fiery furnace once they had been cast into it?

Who is this God who can cause rivers to flow upstream, who can bring drought or floods of rain? Who is this Christ who can probe the eternities of space and yet penetrate the heart of mortals and cause it "to quake" and "pierce them to the very soul?" (3 Nephi 11:3.)

How would we refer to Him if we had been in His presence? Isaiah declared, "His name shall be called Wonderful, Counsellor, The mighty God, The everlasting Father, The Prince of Peace." (Isaiah 9:6.) The Nephites described Him thus: "They saw a Man descending out of heaven; and he was clothed in a white robe; and he came down and stood in the midst of them; and the eyes of the whole multitude were turned upon him, and they durst not open their mouths, even one to another." (3 Nephi 11:8.)

They stood in absolute reverence before the very Son of God. Later they declared:

> The eye hath never seen, neither hath the ear heard, before, so great and marvelous things as we saw and heard Jesus speak unto the Father;
>
> And no tongue can speak, neither can there be written by any man, neither can the hearts of men conceive so great and marvelous things as we both saw and heard Jesus speak; and no one can conceive of the joy which filled our souls at the time we heard him pray for us unto the Father." (3 Nephi 17:16–17.)

In one seemingly obscure record it states: "And when he [Jesus] had said these words, he wept, and the multitude bare record of it." (3 Nephi 17:21.)

Have you ever wondered what feelings would come to the heart of one who witnessed Jesus weep? I have wept often at the tears of others, both of joy and sorrow, pain and suffering. What effect would the tears of Jesus have upon us—this Being with power to create and organize galaxies and yet so filled with compassion that He could weep in behalf of a small flock of His "other sheep"?

The Lord can touch the eyes of our understanding as He did for Joseph Smith and Sidney Rigdon: "The glory of the Lord shown round about [them]. And [they] beheld the glory of the Son, on the right hand of the Father, and received of his fulness." (D&C 76:19–20.) They "saw the holy angels, and them who are sanctified before his throne, worshiping God, and the Lamb, who worship him forever and ever." (Verse 21.) Consequent to this experience, these two prophets declared: "And now, after the many testimonies which have been given of him, this is the testimony, last of all, which we give of him: That he lives! For we saw him, even on the right hand of God; and we heard the voice bearing record that he is the Only Begotten of the Father—that by him, and through him, and of him, the worlds are and were created, and the inhabitants thereof are begotten sons and daughters unto God." (D&C 76:22–24.)

By Him and through Him and of Him the worlds are and were created. His creations continue. Again we ask with childlike innocence, "Who is this Jesus?"

Joseph Smith and Oliver Cowdery described Him in these words:

> The veil was taken from our minds, and the eyes of our understanding were opened.
>
> We saw the Lord standing upon the breastwork of the pulpit, before us; and under his feet was a paved work of pure gold, in color like amber.
>
> His eyes were as a flame of fire; the hair of his head was white like the pure snow; his countenance shone above the brightness of the sun; and his voice was as the sound of the rushing of great waters, even the voice of Jehovah, saying:

I am the first and the last; I am he who liveth, I am he who was slain; I am your advocate with the Father. (D&C 110:1–4.)

Of course His countenance was brighter than the sun! He is the power by which the sun was made; His is the power by which it brings life and light to our planet. He was slain yet lives again; He is our eternal advocate with the Father.

Joseph and Oliver were told, "Behold, your sins are forgiven you; you are clean before me; therefore, lift up your heads and rejoice." (D&C 110:5.)

We do not understand fully how repentance works, but it does work. God, who can behold "worlds pass away," can, through His pure love and atonement, cleanse us from our sins, satisfying justice and extending mercy. Who is this Jesus who can satisfy the demands of justice collectively for all of the children of God who will come unto Him and repent?

Jesus the Christ is Lord and Creator, Redeemer and Atoner, Deliverer and Exemplar, Chief Cornerstone and Judge, King and Lamb of God, Messiah and Comforter, Prophet and Teacher, and the Great Jehovah; He is the only true and Begotten Son of God, our Eternal Father. It is through His almighty power and His limitless love that we "live, and move, and have our being." (Acts 17:28.) It is He who strides the heavens, who oversees and governs the innumerable suns and stars and worlds. In this life, we who have accepted Him as Lord and King and Divine Ruler of our destinies humbly bow in absolute submissiveness before His holy throne and declare, "Hosanna, hosanna to God and the Lamb, forever and forever and forever!"

## CHAPTER FIVE

# The Great Plan of
# Salvation and Exaltation

President Boyd K. Packer assigned the General Authorities to submit to him, in a page and not more than two, the great plan of salvation. The greatest difficulty in the assignment was in reducing to two typewritten pages or less all that we know and understand about this wonderful plan of happiness and salvation. It was a very thought-provoking and learning experience. What you read below is a result of that assignment.

The Lord God spoke to Moses and declared, "For behold, this is my work and my glory—to bring to pass the immortality and eternal life of man." (Moses 1:39.) We received "hope of eternal life, which God, that cannot lie, promised before the world began." (Titus 1:2.) The great plan was presented by God the Father, its author. Elohim had clothed our intelligences which "have no beginning; they existed before, they shall have no end . . . they are . . . eternal" (Abraham 3:18), with spirits like unto the form of mankind in his own image. (See Abraham 4:26–27.)

An earth was formed whereon these spirits were to dwell.

(Abraham 3:21; 4:1.) The plan provided that all of God's spiritual children would come to earth, where God would "prove them . . . to see if they will do all things whatsoever the Lord their God shall command them." (Abraham 3:25.)

God provided us with our first parents, Adam and Eve (Abraham 4:26), who would take upon them physical bodies. They were commanded to be "fruitful and multiply" (Abraham 4:28); thus, "man may be." They transgressed a lesser law in order that the Lord's commandment to multiply might be fulfilled. The transgression brought about a need for a redemption. (Moses 3:17.) The transgression brought death into the world. The Redemption would redeem all mankind. A Savior (Redeemer) was provided to redeem us from the Fall, which Redemption overcame the pain of death. (2 Nephi 9:7.) Our Father in Heaven, knowing that all mankind would sin, provided also for a Savior to atone for our sins and to pay the full cost of redemption for the totality of mankind. (2 Nephi 9:11.)

Justice and mercy were introduced. (2 Nephi 9:12, 17.) However, mercy could not rob justice. If so, "God would cease to be God." (Alma 42:25.) Thus we are assured that "justice exerciseth all his demands, and also mercy claimeth all which is her own; and thus none but the truly penitent are saved." (Mosiah 2:38–39; see also Alma 42:24.) Mercy is extended to those who accept Jesus Christ as the Son of God, exercise faith, perform good works, repent, and are baptized. (2 Nephi 9:23–24.) After we have accepted Christ, we must endure to the end. We must become steadfast and immovable so that we may have everlasting salvation. (Mosiah 5:15; 2 Nephi 9:26.)

"The plan of mercy could not be brought about except an atonement should be made." (Alma 42:15.) The Lord will judge all mankind according to their hearts. (D&C 137:9.) The promise is that those who are washed clean "shall receive a reward according to their works, for they are heirs of salvation," both the living and the deceased. (D&C 138:59; Ephesians 2:4–5; Mosiah 3:26.) Therefore, those who repent and harden not their hearts shall have claim on mercy "through [the] Only Begotten Son" and "shall enter into [His] rest." (Alma 12:34.)

All mankind will be resurrected. (2 Nephi 9:6–7, 10–12.) Before the resurrection, the righteous will be received into a state called paradise. (2 Nephi 9:13.) The wicked will go to a spirit prison, sometimes referred to as hell. (2 Nephi 9:12.)

After the resurrection, a second judgment will take place. All mankind will be consigned to a glory except the sons of perdition. (1 Corinthians 15:40–44.) The sons of perdition will have a second death (D&C 76:32, 37) and will remain embodied but without forgiveness in this world or in the world to come. (D&C 76:34.)

All the rest shall be brought forth . . . to receive a glory. (D&C 76:39–42.) There will be three degrees of glory: telestial, terrestrial, and celestial. Those who inherit the celestial reward will "dwell in the presence of God and his Christ forever and ever." (D&C 76:62.) Those who receive a terrestrial glory will "receive the presence of the Son, but not of the fulness of the Father." (D&C 76:77.) Those who are consigned to a telestial glory are those who are thrust down to hell, who are liars, sorcerers, adulterers, and whoremongers. (D&C 76:84, 103–4.) They will inherit a glory and will receive the administration of angels. (D&C 76:88.)

Those who are baptized, receive the priesthood (if male), receive the temple endowment, are sealed as husbands and wives, and remain true and faithful throughout their lives—these will inherit the highest degree of glory in the celestial kingdom. They will become like God and have eternal lives (that is, eternal increase), "which glory shall be a fulness and a continuation of the seeds forever and ever. Then shall they be gods, because they have no end." (D&C 132:19–20.) "This is the plan of salvation unto all men, through the blood of mine Only Begotten." (Moses 6:62.)

A further study of the following passages would be beneficial also:

*The Great Plan of Salvation and Exaltation*

1 Corinthians 15:22

2 Nephi 2:26; 9:6, 13

Ephesians 2:8

Mosiah 13:28

1 Peter 1:20; 4:6

Alma 12:33

1 John 2:1

Revelation 1:6; 3:21

D&C 45:3

## Chapter Six

# The Master and Emotions

As a Church leader I am exposed every day of every week to marvelous, wonderful, effective people. On the other hand, as General Authorities we meet members who through their conduct have brought the most grievous kinds of consequences into their lives. These sad and sorry experiences test us greatly. It is hard to imagine a transgression or problem that is new or different from what we have seen over and over. Yet somehow it seems to happen each day—always there seems to be some sin or a twist to transgression that we have not encountered before.

After seeing so many experiences of the Saints being tested in every possible way, our own emotions are held under control better.

I want to share with you some of the personal insights that I have discovered always bring about an emotional response that generally involves tears of gladness or sorrow. The Church has a classic video production entitled *How Rare a Possession*. When it was previewed by the Brethren, I was away from the office on a mission tour. Later it was distributed to the stakes, and a special

Sunday night was suggested when the Saints would come together and view it.

The meeting at our stake center was scheduled for 6:00 P.M. I returned home from a stake conference at 5:55 P.M. and went straight to the stake center. President Roylance invited me to sit on the stand. He said, "Would you mind saying a few words when the videotape is over?" Of course I said that I would.

When the time came in the meeting to watch the movie, I went down into the congregation. I will never forget that experience as long as I live. As Vincenzo di Francesca found the Book of Mormon discarded in a waste container—no title page, the name on the cover worn away, some of the pages covered with mold or some other substance—I had an emotional experience. As he cleaned the pages and began to read, my emotions heightened. Somehow my own great love for the Book of Mormon paralleled what I was seeing portrayed on the screen. As Vincenzo stood before the council with absolute integrity and would not put the Book of Mormon aside, burn it, nor cease to read it, I became very emotional.

His life was tried as he went to Australia, to war, back to Italy—always and everlastingly searching for the church that published the book with no name. When he finally discovered the Church, wrote to BYU for information, and then received a reply from President Heber J. Grant, I was more touched. Even after he found the Church, world conditions and other problems kept him from being baptized. Finally, as you recall, Dr. John A. Widtsoe of the Quorum of the Twelve arranged for the local mission president to travel to Vincenzo's village and baptize him. The fulfillment of the accumulated longing and disappointments for years rested upon me. I vicariously knew what that moment of baptism meant to this great man. The tears flowed—I could hardly stop crying. The temple endowment in his life and the conclusion that he died ten years after having gone to the temple, true to his conviction, were overwhelming to me.

As the videotape concluded and I was invited to speak, I had one of the most difficult times I have ever had behind a pulpit. Every particle of my soul was filled with an immense gratitude for God's love for His children. My words were emotional and fell far short of the feelings in my heart. I had been humbled to the dust of the earth and had not the ability to express the feelings of my soul.

Years ago the Church produced another movie entitled *The Windows of Heaven.* I shall never forget the Spirit I felt as I watched Francis Urry portray the part of Lorenzo Snow, this beloved, saintly prophet making his way on primitive transportation the great distance to St. George. It was another emotional experience—the marvelous stake president watering every corn plant by hand from a bucket because a prophet had promised that "the latter rains would come." It took great faith by people who had little else. When the rains came, the little family ran into the rain and knelt in thanks to God with upturned faces.

President Snow, learning of the rain, walking tiredly upstairs where he knelt by his bed and in grand but simple eloquence of gratitude prayed, "Father, please show me something I can do to express my great love for thee." We have experiences like that which are emotional and unforgettable.

Since we have served in the Philippines we have learned much and had many emotional experiences. After a stake conference I was privileged to drive a priesthood leader to his home. It took about two hours. On the way we stopped to visit one of the bishops and saw his humble home. You could put his home inside my office at work. Then we went on to the priesthood leader's home. He was so proud of it. It was old and had block walls and cement floors, and its four or five rooms were meagerly adorned by humble furniture. He introduced me to his family. I signed their scriptures upon request and felt as if I were on the holy ground of God Himself as I stood conversing with them. When I tried to tell my wife about it, I could hardly do it for the emotion. I have been in far more humble homes before many times. I do not know why I became so emotional, except that he was so terribly proud of his home. His entire home would have fit in the living and dining room of our apartment.

A new convert of the Church and her children had not attended Church for several months. The bishop rode out to her home in a jeepney. It took three separate rides to get there. He expected he would find her bitter and unresponsive to his visit and assumed they had gone back to their old ways. The woman warmly welcomed him and took him inside her sweet little nipa hut. She apologized for not coming to church. She said they could not afford the fare for the jeepneys for her and her children. However, she did want the bishop to know they were having family prayer, holding family home evening, studying the scriptures daily, living the Word of Wisdom, and saving their tithing. Then she again humbly apologized for not coming to church.

A recent birthday was my most emotional one. My wife, Merlene, had preceded me back to Salt Lake City. On 26 March, Gale and Carolu Wilson delivered a gift from my wife that she had them hold until my birthday. Along with it was a birthday card. It was simple and inexpensive.

Let me digress for a moment and say it is not easy to be the wife of a General Authority. Many major occurrences and problems happen when I am not around. Even when we are home, our time is not our own. We are called upon to move to distant states and lands. Merlene has had to speak in large regional meetings. Once when I told her she was invited to speak at a regional conference at BYU where there must have been 25,000 or more in the congregation, she said, "I would rather scrub the Marriott Center with a toothbrush than speak there."

The children are often expected to live "General Authority" lives. The whole family is constantly on display. It is not an easy life. I have often wondered if my wife had known when we got married what she knows now whether she would not have selected some wonderful, good man who would work eight hours a day, be home in the evenings, and go to church with her each Sunday.

Now back to the birthday card. I opened the envelope and

read on the front of the card the simple phrase, "With all my love." Inside on the left-hand side were these words, "It means so much to have a love that seems just meant to be." On the right-hand page she had written, "Dear Vaughn." Then these words were on the card: "If I had to do it all over again, I know that I'd choose you. . . . Now that I know the joy that is you, all of the warmth and the love that is you, now that I know how good life can be having you there to share it with me, I know in my heart even more than before, I'd choose you all over again. Happy birthday!" Then these words were written by her: "I guess the greatest, sweetest lessons in this life I have learned from you in a Christ-like way. I love you dearly. Thank you for letting me go home early. Have a great day. All my love, Merlene."

I suppose the reason why it was such a special and emotional experience was that her feelings paralleled mine so exactly.

In the movie *Chariots of Fire,* Eric Lyddel, world-class sprinter from Great Britain, had chosen not to run on Sunday due to his reverence for God and his religion. He was unwilling to compromise his principles even for the leaders of the nation and love of his country. It was decided that he would run in a different event that was scheduled on a day other than Sunday. As he was coming to the mark to get ready to run, Jackson Schultz from the United States slipped a note into his hand that quoted from the Old Testament, "Those who honor God, God will honor." Integrity practiced truly is always an emotional experience for me. Integrity demands enough character and trust in self and God to stand alone in spite of the consequences. We all must do this in our personal lives, business affairs, and families. This is especially true when it costs us something, such as a promotion, image, friends, or future opportunities. There is little testing of our integrity when nothing is lost.

John Yardley is the stake president in Panguitch, Utah. He is a splendid young man who is absolutely pure in heart. He loves youth and children. He loves sports and activities. He came to Philmont Scout Ranch with his family in 1989, as I recall. During the training we showed a videotape produced by the Boy Scouts of America entitled *A Time to Tell*. It is about pedophilia. Often men's perverse behavior leads them to involve boys and young men in sexual indulgences. This videotape portrayed several case studies to demonstrate how a deviant adult might lure young men into a perverted sexual relationship.

In the middle of the videotape John Yardley got up and walked out of the room. After the meeting I said to him, "Is everything all right? Are you okay?" He responded, "I'm fine. I just couldn't stand to watch a man with those evil intentions, even on videotape." He said, "I was getting sick to my stomach; I had to leave." God bless the pure in heart. I became emotional as I thought about this sweet young stake president's purity.

We have a videotape of the movie *Dead Poets Society*. It has been edited for TV use. Robin Williams portrays an English teacher who awakens a sense of experiencing, feeling, and applying poetry in the lives of his students. Most of the students begin to grow and flourish, to feel and sense a great inner awakening of suppressed talents and abilities. But due to the suicide of a young man at school, Robin Williams becomes the whipping boy and is terminated from his teaching position. There are times in the movie when different characters are awakened in various ways. In each of those awakenings I became emotional. At the end of the movie, one young man dares to stand alone and honor his captain—the rejected teacher who had taught him to open his eyes and his heart. His action in turn brought courage to others, who then stand with him.

I wish I could put my finger on what it is that brings great rushes of emotion to my soul. But in my weakness with words, I stand too often helpless. Nonetheless, I would like to share some thoughts and hope that somehow you can feel what I am trying to say.

I always become emotional when I become aware of a truly repentant one. Bravery, loyalty, and integrity in spite of consequence touch me deeply, as do genuine acts of Christian service—

noble and great people stopping to help a child, great leaders who are not above hard and menial labor to serve another; forgiveness by those who truly have something to forgive; someone rescuing another person from a humiliating experience; people who suffer in silence; seeing someone overcome a lifelong habit to join the Church or to become active; watching someone go through the conversion process; observing someone with the "prodigal's" father's compassion; standing alone for right when others buckle under pressure; defending someone who is being criticized but does not deserve the criticism; a truly humble, sincere prayer; sacred music; sincere, humble expressions of gratitude; great concepts and principles.

Abraham Lincoln declared that no enemy or foreign power would ever take one drink out of the Missouri River by force. This statement brings a flood of emotions to me. President Ezra Taft Benson said, "When the second coming takes place, the flag of the United States of America will still be flying over this land." Victor Hugo wrote, "The shepherd does not recoil from the diseased sheep." President Spencer W. Kimball declared, "Make no small plans; they have no magic to stir men's souls." Elder Bruce R. McConkie said, "No other talent exceeds spirituality."

We might well determine that the things which touch us most deeply are the things which we value most. As we are involved in the arts, music, writing, painting, poetry, and the like, we reflect our innermost feelings in what we create. I wrote the following poem as I sat in a zone conference one day. It focuses on the things I love most.

### Who Follow in the Steps He Trod
#### February 5, 1985

I met a man the other day
Who faced endless problems on his way.
His heart was sad, all hope was gone;
He walked in night from dark to dawn.
The emptiness that ruled his life

Remained through all his toil and strife.
The barren deserts seemed less bleak
Than the life he lived from week to week.

The years were multiplied to ten—
I met this selfsame man again.
This time he seemed a different soul:
In every way he had control.
His step was light, his heart was gay,
He always had kind words to say.
He blessed the lives of all he met;
Not one escaped his cast-out net.

The stranger was a welcome friend;
Each broken heart he set to mend.
Nor forgot he still the orphan boy
Or the lonely widow who felt no joy.
No heartsick soul escaped his glance,
Nor did he leave their case to chance.
His worldly wealth he soon spread thin;
No troubled soul he took not in.

And so from dawn to dusk he shared;
All who knew him said he cared.
And so a life of little worth
Became a servant to all the earth.
This empty life we see thus changed
Seemed almost by his God arranged.
And true it is and ever so,
The Master's touch on all below
Who follow in the steps he trod
Will turn the hearts of men to God.

I think we honor our Holy Father and Christ best by serving His children. He honors us most when we serve in a great or small way. The following words are put into verse. I wrote them to reflect my feelings of honoring my Master. He means everything in this

world and more to me. I love Him and honor Him more than
aught else in this world.

MASTER

His realms are those of the heavens;
The earth is His footstool and more.
His mercy is endless and eternal;
His Godhood assured long before.
His countenance shines with pure whiteness,
His eyes like a fire of flame.
He dwells in the Father's bosom;
The Great I Am is His name.

His work is that of the priesthood;
His glory is that of the sun.
His wisdom is greater than wise men;
His justice leaves nothing undone.
His blessings pour down like the rain;
His love is extended to all.
He shepherds us through every trial;
He cradles us close when we fall.

He heals the lame, blind, and leper;
He brings peace to the deeply distressed.
His work is with the orphan and widow;
He seeks out the poor and oppressed.
As the mediator of God, He's rejected;
His ministry was a perpetual strife.
Gethsemane's garden was His great test;
Golgotha's cross cost His life.

His blood flowed like wine from the winepress;
His body was nailed on the cross.
His heart sorrowed almost to breaking
While angels mourned the great loss.
God is His name and God He will be,

His course never changing direction.
His compassion, love, and long-suffering
Reflect in His spotless perfection.

The Redeemer, the Atoner, our Savior,
The Messiah, the Comforter, and Lord.
The Only Begotten of the Father,
The Holy One, our King, and "The Word."
The Rock, our Teacher, our Mediator,
The Exemplar, the Advocate, the Anointed.
Jehovah, Lord God, and Light of the World,
Our Master, Our Christ, God's appointed.

## CHAPTER SEVEN

# To Pray through Christ, Our Advocate

As a young boy going to Primary, I was taught to pray. I did not know how to pray, but I accepted the fact that I should pray. Somehow in my young mind I felt to memorize the Lord's Prayer. Once it was memorized, I used His prayer as though it were mine. At night I would go out on our front porch, then look heavenward and say the Lord's Prayer. If I didn't feel that I was spiritual enough or that my prayer had gotten through, I would simply say it again.

One night I felt I was really praying and that the Lord's Prayer had become mine. All I did was add four additional words, something that multitudes of others have done. As I closed the Lord's Prayer, I said, "For thine is the kingdom, and the power, and the glory, forever" and then added the words, "and forever and ever, amen." I suppose it was a feeling of reverence for God that I was offering in my young mind by adding "and forever and ever."

Thank goodness for prayers that lift us upward even when we are unskilled and untrained but reverent.

During World War II, great lessons were learned in 1943 and 1944. I was a deacon. Many of the young men who had sat at the sacrament table had been drafted or had joined the armed services. The bishopric had a framed board with the names of all of the men and women who were in the military. When a young man was killed in action, a gold star was placed by his name; a white star was placed if he was missing in action; and a red star if he was wounded. Every Sunday I would check out the board, soberly and humbly as any twelve- or thirteen-year-old boy might do. The names represented men and women whom I loved and looked up to. I always felt a deep, penetrating hurt when I would see a new gold, white, or red star by a name.

The Sunday before Thanksgiving a member of our bishopric came to the quorum meeting. He talked about the war and about "our boys" in the service, and then he went to the blackboard. He said, "I hope every young man in this quorum, along with his family, will have a special Thanksgiving prayer on Thursday." Then he asked us what we should express thanks for in our prayer. Of course we all said our country, our freedom; and then individually we made other suggestions, such as the men and women fighting for our country, food, shelter, our flag, and so on. At the close of his discussion, this good man said, "We ought to all remember these things in our Thanksgiving prayer on Thursday."

My heart ached; we had never said a prayer or blessing of any kind in our home. I thought, "Well, I guess we can't have a Thanksgiving prayer at our house." I knew I was too timid and shy to suggest it.

In those days sacrament meeting was at six-thirty on Sunday evening. We had a wonderful sacrament meeting, mostly directed toward Thanksgiving. Near the close of the meeting, our good and wonderful bishop stood up. He talked about our abundant blessings and about the men and women from the ward who were in the military. He tenderly talked about those men who had lost their lives, the wounded, and the missing in action. I remember he talked about liberty and freedom and our country; and then he said, "I hope every single family in this ward will bow in prayer before their Thanksgiving dinner and express gratitude for all we have and this great country and pray that God will help keep us free."

His talk caused a burning desire to pray like I had never felt before. I knew it was hopeless. How could we pray? My dad would probably come home inebriated, if he even came home. I hardly slept Sunday night, worrying about how we could have prayer. It bothered me all day Monday, Tuesday, and Wednesday. Wednesday night my dad did not come home until the middle of the night—drunk. There was a terrible quarrel. That seemed to destroy all hope of having a prayer.

The next morning my four brothers and I went to a nearby field where we could dig a deep hole to work up a terrific appetite. We did not eat breakfast so that we would really be able to stow away the food. With every shovelful of dirt I threw out of the hole, I thought about how we could possibly have a Thanksgiving prayer. I remember thinking that my older brother was brave and not as shy, and maybe he would suggest it. I realize now he probably felt as shy and awkward about asking to pray as I did. We worked up a tremendous appetite.

About two-thirty in the afternoon, our mom called us home and said that dinner was ready. Somehow we had a turkey, mashed potatoes and gravy, hot rolls, yams, dressing, and all else. We all got cleaned up and sat down around the table. Mom and Dad were not speaking to each other. I remember thinking, "Please, God, let us have a prayer. Please somehow let us do what our bishop asked us to do." The food was passed around the table, and then all of a sudden everyone just started to eat. It was too late. I didn't want to eat; I wasn't hungry. I wanted to pray as much as I have ever wanted anything in my life.

That day I made a commitment that no son or daughter of mine would ever want to pray for Thanksgiving and not have that privilege and blessing. As you can imagine, every Thanksgiving prayer is special at our home. We have a twenty-minute program to sing and talk about our country and our freedoms, and then we have a Thanksgiving prayer.

Prayer is not without its hazards, however. Through the years my wife and I and our children have prayed together. One night when Merlene and I were kneeling beside our bed saying our prayers, I was voice—and I was exhausted. Have you ever gone to sleep when you were voice during a prayer? Well, I did on this night. All of a sudden I awoke and heard Merlene laughing. With all the dignity I could muster, I concluded our prayer. When I finished, I asked her, "What were you laughing at?" She said, "When I heard you say 'and God bless Paul [our youngest son] with life, liberty, and the pursuit of happiness,' I knew you were gone."

As a young man I memorized the Sermon on the Mount. The Sermon on the Mount is the greatest sermon ever given. When you memorize something, it is as though it becomes part of you. The difficulty is in making time to regularly review all you memorize so it is not slowly forgotten. Forty years later I still essentially have the Sermon on the Mount memorized, although it might not be in the correct order; however, its principles and message are still fresh in my mind.

In this great and wonderful message, the Master said this about prayer:

> And when thou prayest, thou shalt not be as the hypocrites are: for they love to pray standing in the synagogues and in the corners of the streets, that they may be seen of men. Verily I say unto you, They have their reward.
>
> But thou, when thou prayest, enter into thy closet, and when thou hast shut thy door, pray to thy Father which is in secret; and thy Father which seeth in secret shall reward thee openly.
>
> But when ye pray, use not vain repetitions, as the heathen do: for they think that they shall be heard for their much speaking.
>
> Be not ye therefore like unto them: for your Father knoweth what things ye have need of, before ye ask him.

After this manner therefore pray ye: Our Father which art in heaven, Hallowed be thy name.

Thy kingdom come. Thy will be done in earth, as it is in heaven.

Give us this day our daily bread.

And forgive us our debts, as we forgive our debtors.

And lead us not into temptation, but deliver us from evil: For thine is the kingdom, and the power, and the glory, for ever. Amen.

For if ye forgive men their trespasses, your heavenly Father will also forgive you:

But if ye forgive not men their trespasses, neither will your Father forgive your trespasses. (Matthew 6:5–15.)

When we pray in secret, "the Father seeth in secret and shall reward [us] openly." The Lord expressly instructs us not to use "vain repetitions, as the heathen," and I would add "as some Christians do," "for they think they will be heard for their much speaking." It sounds as if the Master has two concerns about repetition. The first is *vain* repetition. I assume that this refers to saying the same thing in every prayer without thought or feeling. The poet said:

> You might as well pray to a God of stone
> As offer to the living God a prayer of words alone.

In any conversation, who would have much interest if the same phrases and statements were made over and over again without even concentrating the mind on them? I have memorized much—verses, scripture, poetry, and the like. I can rehearse them to myself and think other thoughts at the same time. While my mind is reviewing one thing, I find that I can also consider what I am going to rehearse next or review something on my schedule. (Sometimes if I do this too intensely, I find myself mentally stumbling over what I am rehearsing.) I think we have all had the experience of saying one thing and thinking something else.

Unfortunately, our prayers can be much like that. We may be saying the words in a prayer, but much of our concentration is elsewhere. Sometimes we cannot remember whether we even prayed.

It has been my experience that I often pray more thoughtfully in public. This is especially true when I have been called upon to pray at general conference or in meetings with the other General Authorities. The reason why the Savior disapproved of the hypocrites' prayers, it appears, was that their motivation was wrong: "They love to pray standing in the synagogues and in the corners of the streets, that they may be seen of men." (Matthew 5:5.) Prayers we offer publicly are, for most of us, a real challenge. I think we are not so much interested in impressing people as in trying not to be embarrassed or thoughtless. In the Church, I firmly believe that few prayers are offered with the intent of impressing people more than God. Perhaps this is because we have the true concept of God and His Only Begotten Son, Jesus Christ. When we have God's image in our mind while we are praying, we are more thoughtful, humble, meek, and charitable. As we close our prayers in the name of Jesus Christ and we consider that He is our Master, our Advocate, the one spotless Lamb in all of humanity, then vanity and pride flee from us.

We ought to be aware of our prayers when we pray publicly. We should consider our thoughts and purposes and make certain we pray in reverent humility. We have not instructed the Saints much in public prayer. There is a need to teach a few principles. Elder Bruce R. McConkie said, "The present practice in the Church is the interpretation of the doctrine." Following are guidelines to consider when we pray in conferences, sacrament meetings, and other public or church activities:

- Prayers in sacrament meeting and stake conference should generally not exceed two minutes.
- We do *not* commence our prayers with the statement "Let us pray."
- We specifically pray for the fulfillment of the purposes of that particular meeting, that is, we pray that we will partake

of the sacrament worthily, that the speakers will be inspired, that we will desire to go to the temple, or that we will better prepare for missions. We want to pray for the members and those who have special needs. We need to be aware of the time. Prayer is not a sermon or a call to repentance. It is a sacred communication with God.

• We avoid the more familiar terms of *you* and *your*. When we address Deity in prayer, we use *Thee, Thou, Thy, Thine.* Addressing God our Father in this way shows great respect and reverence.

• The person giving the opening prayer should be on the stand at the commencement of the meeting.

• The congregation should say a loud amen at the conclusion of a talk, sermon, or prayer. President Harold B. Lee said, "It is spiritual applause." A loud amen is our acceptance and our involvement in the prayer. The person saying the prayer is praying in behalf of all of those who are in attendance.

Now, the Lord taught us to pray in secret. What happens to us when we pray in secret? First, our faith is put to the test. How foolish people would feel who pray alone and really do not believe in God. We can pray in public and people might think we believe, but praying alone takes faith. When we pray alone, there is no one to impress with our command of the language, with our beautiful phrases or eloquence. We simply talk with a loving, interested Father about what is troubling us most. We take problems that no one else, not another living soul, can help us with. We become like little children, feeling a dependence and need for someone wiser and with power and influence. We do not have to worry about embarrassment if our prayers are not answered the way we think they should be, because only we and God know for what we pray. When tears come, there is no embarrassment. We can be totally honest, knowing that we cannot lie to or deceive the Spirit or God. He knows us for our real worth. He knows who and what we really are, not what we seem to be. When we have personal problems or struggles, we can pray and know that these things are kept totally confidential. We can discuss our weaknesses, our sins, our frustrations, our needs, and know that He will listen and respond.

We can learn a great deal about a person by the way he or she prays in private. A hurried, get-it-done attitude in private prayer shows a lack of reverence for God and demonstrates that perhaps that person does pray to be heard of men.

The hymn recalls, "There is an hour of peace and rest, unmarred by earthly care; 'tis when before the Lord I go, and kneel in secret prayer." The last verse reminds us of the comfort we receive: "When thorns are strewn along my path, and foes my feet ensnare, my Savior to my aid will come, if sought in secret prayer." (Hans Peterson, "Secret Prayer," *Hymns,* no. 144.)

The Lord also taught the righteous Nephites who had gathered at the temple in Bountiful how to pray, as recorded in 3 Nephi 13:9: "Our Father who art in heaven." With our understanding, we pray "*who* art in heaven," not "*which* art in heaven" (see Matthew 6:9). Our concept of God teaches us this simple truth. Continuing, we pray, "Hallowed be thy name." In Matthew the phrase "Thy kingdom come" precedes "Thy will be done," but this phrase is missing in 3 Nephi. It commences instead, "Thy will be done on earth as it is in heaven." (Verse 10.) What a blessing if all people truly prayed that God's will would be done on earth! That will happen sometime in the not-too-distant future. What a glorious day that will be! This sentence also teaches us about heaven. God's will is done in heaven. What a blessing to know that God, with absolute knowledge and wisdom, who understands justice and mercy, will have His will done in heaven.

We are taught in Matthew to pray for food: "Give us this day our daily bread." (Verse 11.) This is not included in 3 Nephi. One woman I met in the Philippines said, "I am glad I am poor; I have to depend on God every day to provide food for my family." It is appropriate to pray for food.

"And forgive us our debts, as we forgive our debtors." (Verse 12.) Much of the heartache in the world and in the Church comes to those who are unable to do this. We pray "forgive us our debts" and leave the rest of the sentence unspoken.

In the Sermon on the Mount, the Savior taught, "Blessed are the merciful: for they shall obtain mercy." (Matthew 5:7.) And in this dispensation, He further stated, "I, the Lord, will forgive whom I will forgive, but of you it is required to forgive all men." (D&C 64:10.) This is a beautiful phrase in the prayer, "Forgive us our debts," the qualifier being "as we forgive our debtors."

"And lead us not into temptation, but deliver us from evil." (Verse 13.) Joseph Smith corrected the phrase to read "and suffer us not to be led into temptation." It is actually exactly the same in 3 Nephi 13:12 as in Matthew. It should not test anyone's faith but should be an additional witness of the Book of Mormon. The Savior gave identical counsel on both continents. Joseph's translation simply clarifies it for us.

Next the Savior taught that we need to pray to be delivered from evil. In Mosiah 4:29, King Benjamin instructs, "And finally, I cannot tell you all the things whereby ye may commit sin; for there are divers ways and means, even so many that I cannot number them." Then in verse 30 he counsels, "Watch yourselves, and your thoughts, and your words, and your deeds, and observe the commandments of God, and continue in the faith." In this one phrase, "Deliver us from evil," we ask the Lord to keep us from all the ways we may sin.

Finally the Master gives us the assurance of the authority of God: "For thine is the kingdom, and the power, and the glory, forever." (Verse 13.) How small we are in our relationship to Him, and yet we are His children with seeds of divinity and potentiality in us to become like Him. His love for us is eternal and limitless; it is unconditional and will reach out to all.

The Lord's Prayer is simple yet profound. A child can understand its phrases. The intellectual can be challenged by its implications and the profound truths found therein.

James Montgomery seems to catch the spirit of humble prayer in these words:

Prayer is the soul's sincere desire,
Uttered or unexpressed,
The motion of a hidden fire
That trembles in the breast.

Prayer is the burden of a sigh,
The falling of a tear,
The upward glancing of an eye
When none but God is near.

("PRAYER IS THE SOUL'S SINCERE DESIRE,"
*HYMNS,* NO. 145.)

What a marvelous spiritual revival we would have if the Saints would pray sincerely and humbly to God—the One Being in all of eternity who is available to every soul who walks the earth, every moment of every day. None are exempt save it be by their conduct and choosing. Oh, how we ought to love and worship our God and His Son. Oh, what an answer to the trials, frustrations, and perplexities of life. Peace and blessings come to the contrite soul who approaches God with a broken heart.

This is also what the Savior taught in the parable of the two men who went up to the temple to pray, describing the publican as "standing afar off, [he] would not lift up so much as his eyes unto heaven, but smote upon his breast, saying, God be merciful to me a sinner."

The Lord described this man as going "down to his house justified." (Luke 18:13–14.)

Let us be most earnest, humble, sincere, forgiving, and filled with charity as we pray. Peace will come, answers will be given, promises will be fulfilled; and the soul will be satisfied. Prayer is the righteous soul's sincere desire.

## Chapter Eight

# Christ, the Light of
# Worlds without Number

I'd like to begin this chapter with a review of some figures discussed in an earlier chapter. (See chapter 4, "Who Is This Jesus?") One million seconds is twelve days. One billion seconds is thirty-two years, and a trillion seconds is 32,000 years. With the naked eye we can see approximately 5,000 stars on a clear night when there is no moon. With a pair of binoculars we can see nearly 50,000 stars. Using a high-powered telescope we can see beyond the Milky Way galaxy. The earth is part of the Milky Way galaxy. We are on the far outside edge. Astronomers tell us that the Milky Way galaxy has 600 billion stars and is something like 400 billion miles across. They have identified twenty-one other galaxies as large as the Milky Way and suggest there may be as many as hundreds of billions of galaxies. The mind of man can hardly wrap itself around such thoughts or possibilities.

W. W. Phelps understood in a profound way what the world does not yet understand. Consider the powerful concepts in his lyrics:

If you could hie to Kolob
In the twinkling of an eye,
And then continue onward
With that same speed to fly,
Do you think that you could ever,
Through all eternity,
Find out the generation
Where Gods began to be?

Or see the grand beginning,
Where space did not extend?
Or view the last creation,
Where Gods and matter end?
Methinks the Spirit whispers,
"No man has found 'pure space,'
Nor seen the outside curtains,
Where nothing has a place."

The works of God continue,
And worlds and lives abound;
Improvement and progression
Have one eternal round.
There is no end to matter;
There is no end to space;
There is no end to spirit;
There is no end to race.

("IF YOU COULD HIE TO KOLOB,"
*HYMNS,* NO. 284.)

The Hubble telescope can probe 14 billion light years into space. Imagine that! Consider that light travels at 186,000 miles a second. Multiply 186,000 by 60 seconds by 60 minutes by 24 hours by 365.25 days, and that is one light year. Do you know how far 14 billion light years actually is? One day I figured it out. It is approximately 82 trillion, 175 billion million actual miles, or almost

900,000 times the distance to the sun. The sun is 93,000,000 miles from the earth.

Scientists and astronomers have supposedly been able to identify black holes. The *Washington Post* stated, "A black hole is thought to be a collapsing object (such as a star) whose gravitational pull is so powerful that nothing—not even light—can come out again once it has crossed the hole's threshold." The same article suggests, "Evidence reveals a black hole 3 million times the mass of the sun lurking in earth's backyard." The article claims that the Hubble telescope and the Compton gamma ray observatory have used advanced technology to reveal evidence of at least a dozen black holes. (*Pacific Stars and Stripes,* June 2, 1992.)

The prophets Enoch, Abraham, and Joseph Smith have unquestionably understood more about the celestial realms of the extensive heavens than all the noted astronomers from time immemorial. Imagine if we could discern the wonders of the universe with spiritual eyes aided by the powers of God. What have the prophets known? What have they understood?

In section 88 of the Doctrine and Covenants, the Prophet Joseph recorded "the Lord's message of peace to us," also called "the olive leaf." In this great revelation we begin to discern the smallest part of the eternal power and authority of the Savior, both in this world and the galaxies beyond. It is difficult for us to comprehend the majesty of Christ. As we consider galaxies and stars, light and black holes, the earth and other planets, we must consider the power of Him who made them.

> He that ascended up on high, as also he descended below all things, in that he comprehended all things, that he might be in all and through all things, the light of truth;
>
> Which truth shineth. This is the light of Christ. As also he is in the sun, and the light of the sun, and the power thereof by which it was made.
>
> As also he is in the moon, and is the light of the moon, and the power thereof by which it was made;

As also the light of the stars, and the power thereof by which they were made;

And the earth also, and the power thereof, even the earth upon which you stand.

And the light which shineth, which giveth you light, is through him who enlighteneth your eyes, which is the same light that quickeneth your understandings;

Which light proceedeth forth from the presence of God to fill the immensity of space—

The light which is in all things, which giveth life to all things, which is the law by which all things are governed, even the power of God who sitteth upon his throne, who is in the bosom of eternity, who is in the midst of all things. (D&C 88:6–13.)

No wonder we come to temples for *light* and knowledge. Temples are "Holiness to the Lord" edifices dedicated to the Savior. He is "the light of the sun, the moon, and the stars, and the very power thereof by which they were made." Imagine the "light proceedeth forth from the presence of God to fill the immensity of space. The light which is in all things, which giveth life to all things, by which all things are governed, even by the power of God."

Considering the source of all truth and light, is it possible that truth can have a tangible effect upon us? It does. "The Spirit giveth light to every man that cometh into the world; and the Spirit enlighteneth every man through the world, that hearkeneth to the voice of the Spirit." (D&C 84:46.)

Thus we see that light cleaveth unto light and truth cleaveth unto truth. Mankind can receive light. The Lord said, "And if your eye be single to my glory, your whole bodies shall be filled with light." (D&C 88:67.) In Proverbs we read that "the spirit of man is the candle of the Lord." (Proverbs 20:27.) Righteous men and women do give off an aura of light. At a funeral service once I heard President Hugh B. Brown say, "Death is not the end; it is putting out the candle because the dawn has come." Compare the light of a candle to the immensity and glory of the dawning of a new day. Surely our light is limited compared to the light of Christ; nevertheless, He said to His disciples, "Ye are the light of the world. A city that is set on an hill cannot be hid. Neither do men light a candle, and put it under a bushel, but on a candlestick; and it giveth light unto all that are in the house. Let your light so shine before men, that they may see your good works, and glorify your Father which is in heaven." (Matthew 5:14–16.)

We begin to understand how light works when we have "spiritually been born of God . . . [and] received his image in [our] countenance." (Alma 5:14.)

Those who are worthy when they attend the temple have His image in their countenance. His light is in them and through them. When they choose to be obedient, to sustain and follow the prophets of the living God, the light reaches into their marital relations, family responsibilities, Church callings, and workday activities.

The light and understanding that our temples provide regarding marriage alone are wonderful. A young couple gave birth to a son. They named him "Amazing," hoping that somehow he would live up to his name and do something great. Actually, he never did. In fact, all that he did was rather mundane. He never really accomplished anything great. He married, lived on the family farm, raised a family, and was the brunt of jokes all his life because of his name.

Finally, as he grew old, he said to his wife, "When I die, please do not put my name on the gravemarker; maybe that will stop all the jokes." Later he died, and she was true to her promise but decided she ought to have something inscribed. She had them put, "Here lies a man who for sixty years loved and was faithful to his wife." And now people read the inscription, then point and say, "That's amazing." Marriages in the temple endure not just for sixty years but for an eternity.

That person who responds to and is filled with the light of Christ can be a marvelous influence for good. "The glory of God is intelligence, or, in other words, light and truth." (D&C 93:36.) We receive light and truth in the holy temples, not only through the endowment but also from the light and intelligence that flow naturally to us as we seek the "blessings of the fathers." (Abraham 1:2.)

Light comes to us from God in many ways. In the dedicatory prayer at the Kirtland Temple, Joseph Smith prayed (which prayer was given to him by revelation): "And in a manner that we may be found worthy, in thy sight, to secure a fulfillment of the promises which thou hast made unto us, thy people, in the revelations given unto us; That thy glory may rest down upon thy people, and upon this thy house, which we now dedicate to thee, that it may be sanctified and consecrated to be holy, and that thy holy presence may be continually in this house." (D&C 109:11–12.)

Consider the words that increase our light and knowledge such as *revelation, glory, intelligence, glorious tidings, truth, holiness, shine forth as fair as the moon and clear as the sun; our garments may be made pure, spotless, white;* and even the *bright shining seraphs.* Seraphim are angelic beings mentioned in Isaiah's vision. Cherubim, according to the LDS Bible Dictionary, are figures representing heavenly creatures. Angels, including cherubim and seraphim, are beings of light.

Orson F. Whitney said:

> Latter-day Saints, it was for this purpose that you gathered to Zion. Young men and young women of this people, it was for this purpose that you were born upon this favored land, the land upon which God intends to build the city of Zion, to erect His holy Temple, upon which the glory of God will rest, and reflect from the towers of the city, from the spires of the Temple, from the hearts and minds of the pure, the noble and the righteous, to give joy to all the world. Then will be fulfilled the words of the Prophet Isaiah, who spake concerning Zion:
>
> "Arise, shine; for thy light is come, and the glory of the Lord is risen upon thee. For, behold, the darkness shall cover

the earth, and gross darkness the people: but the Lord shall arise upon thee, and his glory shall be seen upon thee. And the Gentiles shall come to thy light, and kings to the brightness of thy rising." (Isaiah 60:1–3.)

This is no dream, brethren and sisters. It is no whim or fancy of men. It is an inspired utterance, the heaven-born thought of a holy man of God, who spake as he was moved upon by the Holy Ghost. And this is a portion of the destiny of this people—to build up such a Zion; and not only to build a city—that I conceive to be a comparatively insignificant portion of the great mission devolving upon us—but to prepare a people, the pure in heart, for the coming of the Lord Jesus to reign in His glory. ("Zion and Her Redemption," Discourse, September 22, 1889.)

In my mind I see the darkness of the whole earth and one great shining city of light, a city that will be a light to the world. The light will start with our temples and radiate into the hearts of the people, and this people will then be a light to the world. That city will be Salt Lake City and its suburbs—east, west, north, and south. There is sublime joy as we obtain light. The law of the Lord shall go forth from Zion through His holy prophets and apostles, and none shall prevail against them. The faithful Saints will gather as modern Israel and dispel the darkness of the world. Truly—

> The morning breaks, the shadows flee;
> Lo, Zion's standard is unfurled!
> The dawning of a brighter day,
> Majestic rises on the world.
>
> (PARLEY P. PRATT, "THE MORNING BREAKS,"
> HYMNS, NO. 1)

I thank God for the light I have received from the prophets, from the Book of Mormon, from the commandments, and from our "Holiness to the Lord" edifices. This is God's work, and all is light and truth through His Holy Son, Jesus the Christ.

## CHAPTER NINE

# The Incomparable Christ,
# His Disciples, and Easter Morn

One dimension of those who truly possess charity is that they will come to the aid of those who are humiliated, embarrassed, shy, or timid.

When our son Paul was a senior high school student, he was running for senior class president. One day during the lunch hour, a student came through the lunch line at the cafeteria. As she came to the dining room, she tripped and fell into her tray of food. Many of the students around her began to laugh and make comments. It was an extremely humiliating experience. Paul went to her, helped her up, wiped off her clothes, reached into his pocket, and gave her his dollar for lunch money. He told her that he would clean up the floor and suggested she go get another tray of food. The student left the place of embarrassment, and Paul cleaned up the mess. We assume he went without lunch that day.

Paul never told us about this experience; we got a phone call from a mother in our ward whose daughter had seen it take place. I was humbled and felt I would rather have Paul do that any day than be elected to a position based largely on popularity and school politics.

In a special book I have, *Happy Homes and the Hearts That Make Them*, Samuel Smiles relates an experience in the life of Sir Walter Scott.

> Sir Walter Scott was a gentleman's gentleman. He was successful and had a marvelous reputation. Men of high position enjoyed being with him and sought him out. He made them feel important and always lifted those with whom he met or conversed. Women of any station felt at ease with him and secure in his presence. People gravitated to him. Nor was it just adults; youth and children were likewise attracted to this noble man and never felt intimidated or ill at ease. They loved being with him, and he communicated on their level with such elegant simplicity that they adored him.
>
> Someone asked him how it was that he had such a special way with everyone and anyone he met. Said the inquirer, " You must have had a wonderful mother who taught you to love and enjoy people." Sir Walter Scott confessed that he had a wonderful mother but said that he had learned how to love and serve people from an experience in his boyhood. A stray dog was in the neighborhood. Young Walter decided he would scare it away. He picked up a large stone and threw it at the dog. He had not intended to hit the dog but rather to frighten it. The rock hit one of the dog's legs and broke it. The dog fell to its knees, crawled up to young Walter, and licked his shoes. He learned from a stray dog the great lesson of his feelings for people. (P. 515.)

Vorris Tenney, a former mission president and descendant of Jacob Hamblin, told us the following experience as related by Jacob Hamblin, I believe:

> A little girl, a daughter of a family crossing the plains, had one precious possession that she loved with all her heart. It

was a stick doll. The mother had made a little dress and bonnet for it. She held it to her bosom, she cradled and cuddled it constantly. One morning before the wagons began to move, the little girl played with her doll, then she put it to sleep in a little bed of pine branches and leaves. She forgot the doll as the wagons rolled westward. That night she cried uncontrollably. The father came back to her. He took her in his arms and kissed her and loved her and said, "Don't worry, honey; I will go back and get your doll." He left immediately and walked the 15 miles back to retrieve her doll and then returned the 15 miles and arrived back to the wagon train just before dawn. He presented his daughter with her doll and prepared to "move out" with the rest of the wagon train.

The greatness in that story comes as you ponder the situation. Here was a man, a real pioneer, who would have worked and walked almost to exhaustion every single day. When we become exhausted and fatigue takes over, our bodies plead for rest. Mentally we waver; we lack enthusiasm, strength, and commitment; we need rest.

The doll was of little economic value—a substitute could have been made. A great deal of justifiable rationalization could have been considered. How deep is the love of a sweet, gentle father who would walk thirty miles when he was exhausted to soothe his brokenhearted little daughter! This is one of the sweet stories of sacrifice that will never make it into the popular history books where great and mighty deeds are recorded. But I promise you it will be emblazoned in gold on Judgment Day, and a little girl who grew up will never forget a father's love for her.

All of these examples of love, charity, and service lead into why we celebrate Easter. Christ's entire ministry came to one pivotal moment in time, a time that would include Gethsemane, scourging, abuse, scorn, and Golgotha's cross. The above are examples of wonderful Saints who suffer and sacrifice following His lonely example.

Easter morning is the one time when heaven's veil seems most transparent. The celebration of the Resurrection is as irresistible as the dawning of a new day. President Ezra Taft Benson stated, "The greatest events of history are those that affect the greatest number for the longest periods. By this standard, no event could be more important to individuals or nations than the resurrection of the Master." (*Come Unto Christ* [Salt Lake City: Deseret Book Co., 1983], p. 4.) The Resurrection involves all mankind. Easter Sunday is a time of triumph and jubilation. It is a time of rejoicing and celebration. It is a time of renewed life springing forth. Buds burst forth from branches in their time of awakening. Most of us, the believer and unbeliever alike, feel something special about Easter. It may well be that the Light of Christ that enlightens every person brings remembrance to our spirits of that glorious day of our Lord's resurrection.

On that day nearly two millennia ago, surely all the hosts of heaven—those who had not yet come to earth as well as those who had already experienced mortality—shouted with eternal praises for our Lord Jehovah. The Resurrection is of such consequence that every spiritual child of God must knowingly and unknowingly feel a swelling of rapture. The gift is to all.

On Easter morning we wash and scrub ourselves clean, we put on our best—sometimes a new Easter outfit—and we go to church. Always to the believer, Easter Sunday is a memorable one. We prepare for Easter. Now contemplate with me the Master's preparation.

Isaiah foretold the Resurrection: "He will swallow up death in victory; and the Lord God will wipe away tears from off all faces." (Isaiah 25:8.) Job, in his powerful testimony, proclaimed words that have endured through the centuries: "Oh that my words were now written! oh that they were printed in a book! That they were graven with an iron pen and lead in the rock for ever! For I know that my redeemer liveth, and that he shall stand at the latter day upon the earth: And though after my skin worms destroy this body, yet in my flesh shall I see God." (Job 19:23–26.)

Job used the term *redeemer*. He knew that Jesus would redeem us from the grave. He also knew that he (Job) would see this Christ in the latter days.

During the latter part of His ministry, the Savior knew that His time was short. "From that time forth began Jesus to shew unto his disciples, how that he must go unto Jerusalem, and suffer many things of the elders and chief priests and scribes, and be killed, and be raised again the third day." (Matthew 16:21.)

We cannot fathom the mind of the Christ, but we sense again a loneliness and abandonment which He must have felt during His final hours. He prophesied that He would be betrayed and be crucified. (See Matthew 20:19.) Days before the crucifixion took place, He told of the manner of death He would suffer. As He pondered the things that would transpire in the last hours of His life, it appears that He was troubled most by His false accusers, including Judas, the chief priest, and the scribes. (See Matthew 20:18.)

The Master could have been preoccupied with the coming, ominous events that would test even the Son of God. Somehow in the compression of the activities during the Master's final hours, He still reached out with compassion.

As the company left Jericho, two blind men sitting by the wayside heard that Jesus had passed. They cried out, "Have mercy on us, O Lord, thou Son of David. And the multitude rebuked them, . . . but they cried the more saying, Have mercy on us, O Lord, thou Son of David. And Jesus stood still, and called them, and said, What will ye that I shall do unto you? They say unto him, Lord, that our eyes may be opened. So Jesus had compassion on them, and touched their eyes: and immediately their eyes received sight." (Matthew 20:30–34.)

We assume these men had been blind from birth. Imagine that the first person they saw after having received their sight was the Son of God. Consider the dual sensation of being able to see and then beholding the Christ. The Savior knew of their suffering, worthiness, and simple faith. He granted the blessing immediately. Someone said, "You can see further through a teardrop than a telescope." Surely joy and tears, happiness and exquisite relief rushed into their souls. The final sentence in Matthew 20 states, "And they [the two blind men] followed him."

Now, Jesus' triumphal entry to Jerusalem was next. A great multitude spread their garments in the way; others cut down branches from the trees and strewed them in the way.

The throngs and multitude of people went before Him, and others followed. All cried out in honor of Him, "Hosanna to the Son of David: Blessed is he that cometh in the name of the Lord; Hosanna in the highest." (Matthew 21:9.) We refer to this as His triumphal entry into Jerusalem. The believers banded together to declare their allegiance and to call Him the prophet of Nazareth. (Verse 11.) His indignation against the profiteers, "all them that sold and bought in the temple" (verse 12), caused Him to overthrow the tables of the moneychangers and other merchants. This temple was His holy house, a "Holiness to the Lord" edifice. We imagine the power of the rebuke by the lawful owner and the subsequent anger of those who had perverted the rites of the temple. They would become enemies.

However, "the blind and the lame came to him in the temple" and were healed. (Verse 14.) "The chief priests and scribes saw the wonderful things that he did, and the children crying in the temple, and saying, Hosanna." (Verse 15.) Such an experience should melt the heart of the hardest disbeliever. Imagine the majesty of the miracle of seeing the lame walk and the blind see. What profound joy to those healed as well as their families and loved ones, yet the chief priests and scribes were extremely displeased. Satan had power over them, and they resented the miracles Jesus wrought.

Jesus later described those scribes and Pharisees. He said they "sit in Moses' seat" (Matthew 23:2), which "connotes a chair of judgment and instruction" (footnote 2b in the Latter-day Saint edition of the King James Version of the Bible). He further said, "They bind heavy burdens and grievous to be borne, and lay them on men's shoulders; but they themselves will not move them with one of their fingers." (Verse 4.) Further, they do works to be seen of men, love the uppermost rooms and the chief seats, and shut up the kingdom of heaven against men; they devour widows' houses, and for pretence make long prayers, act as hypocrites who pay tithing but neglect the weightier matters, strain at a goat and swallow a camel, and commit extortion and excess. Incredibly, the Master still loves those listed above. What does it take to understand and comprehend the condescensions of Christ? He enabled every soul who ever lives in this second estate to be resurrected—a universal gift of God provided through His justice and mercy.

The Master gave His life, a spotless offering, for all mankind. Even sons of perdition will be resurrected. We proclaim it is only just that men should not be held accountable for Adam's transgression—thus the Atonement and Crucifixion, leading to the full redemption of the Fall for all humanity. We cannot comprehend this priceless gift. If we did, we would surely stand in absolute awe at the wonders of the Resurrection. It is glorious to think of a resurrected body free from pain, illness, disease, aging, or deformity. There must be other side benefits to the Resurrection that would thrill us. With a resurrected body, our minds will undoubtedly function better; our comprehension, understanding, memory, recollection, knowledge, retention, intelligence, and wisdom will all be enhanced.

With a resurrected body, we will be relieved of the present limitations placed on us; we will move and act and feel quicker, better, and more deeply. Our love and compassion will be expanded; our fears and frustrations will be lessened. All of our senses of touch, sight, hearing, tasting, and smelling will improve beyond our comprehension. Life in a resurrected body will be glorious.

These gifts all come from a loving Christ. Even those who inherit the telestial kingdom would hardly dare believe the joys and beauties that await them by and by. Even those who ridiculed and rejected their Savior will have the glorious blessing of resurrection.

The final hours of the Master's life bring much into focus for His disciples. The sacrament was instituted by the Lord Himself. Of all the ordinances in the Church, baptism and partaking of the sacrament tie most closely to the Atonement. Would to God that every member of this Church could understand the sacramental ordinance. Those who live the gospel from week to week, who do not commit transgressions serious enough to bring them before a common judge, have a continuous opportunity to be forgiven. All who partake of the sacrament with humble hearts and contrite spirits, who may have erred or offended during the week, can find forgiveness. Of course, repentance is also required to obtain forgiveness for each sin. Each member who renews his or her covenants through the sacrament feels the healing blessing of forgiveness. Each week we strive for a slightly loftier level of Christlike living. We need not be baptized every year or two to receive continued forgiveness. We need only approach the sacramental ordinance in a contrite, repentant, humble way in order to receive the forgiveness we desire.

In his final hours, the Master washed the feet of His apostles, including Judas.

> Ye call me Master and Lord: and ye say well; for so I am.
>
> If I then, your Lord and Master, have washed your feet; ye also ought to wash one another's feet.
>
> For I have given you an example, that ye should do as I have done to you.
>
> Verily, verily, I say unto you, The servant is not greater than his lord. (John 13:13–16.)

How often have we read the words "a new commandment I give unto you"? The Ten Commandments had sounded down through the millennia since Moses' time, and now an additional commandment came from the Master: "That ye love one another; as I have loved you, that ye also love one another." (John 13:34.)

Only those who are true possessors of charity can measure up to the full stature of this new commandment. This is the commandment that lifts us to the more noble and virtuous life. We cannot nor ever will love one another as He has loved us until we exercise in our own lives the full dimensions of charity. Those who practice charity may not always receive the promised benefits and ultimate successes. Ours is a different time schedule, but by and by we will all learn and know that "charity never faileth." (1 Corinthians 13:8.) The pure love of Christ will eventually triumph over all the evils, including power, pride, boasting, worldly acclaim, cruelty, wars, perversion, sadness, and heartache. The Lord through His servants has promised that charity will never fail. One day charity, the pure love of Christ, will triumph over all the world. Those who are possessors of charity will triumph over all evil and will dwell with the author of this "new commandment" forever and forever.

Before the Master's mortal life was over, He would teach his disciples of His Father's house and the many mansions that He would prepare for them. He promised that the Comforter whom the Father would send would teach them all things and bring all things to their remembrance. Again, the Holy Ghost was sent in His name. Is it little wonder the penalty is so severe for those who deny the Holy Ghost?

The Master taught them about peace, the true vine, greater love, prayer and intercession, unity, and sanctification; then the hour for Gethsemane arrived. He went over the brook Kedron, where there was a garden into which He entered. It is doubtful that any living soul will ever comprehend the least particle of suffering in Gethsemane. The collective balance of all of the evil, hurt, suffering, illnesses, and sicknesses of every being was on one arm of the scale demanding justice; and Jesus, the Son of God, satisfying every slightest demand of that justice, was on the other. Justice was satisfied for all those who truly come unto Him and keep His commandments. There is hardly any more beautiful concept on the earth than mercy and justice fully satisfied, fulfilled, and extended to the righteous.

President J. Reuben Clark said in essence that when the Lord metes out punishment for the things we do wrong, He will mete out the least possible punishment to satisfy justice, and when He metes out blessings for the things we do right, He will mete out the greatest blessings possible. (Conference Report, April 1958, pp. 48–49.)

As discussed elsewhere in this book, Gethsemane was the most severe experience of pain, suffering, and mental agony ever experienced. (See chapter 3, "The Master, the Winepress, and Us.") The demands physically, mentally, and spiritually were incomparable to any ever known in eternity. The magnificent Christ not only endured the physical trials, more than man can bear, but indeed also had reserve strength to continue through the last trying hours of His life. He was examined, mistreated, abused, scourged, mocked, and judged. His final treading of the winepress came on the cross. Compassion was His even in the darkest hour of His life. It was, as Shakespeare said, "the thousand natural shocks that flesh is heir to" (Hamlet 3.1.62–63) or, as Crowell stated, "All the ills that men endure." It was all this and much, much more. Finally, it was finished. Jesus Christ, Jehovah, Lord God, laid down His life of His own volition.

> But Mary stood without at the sepulchre weeping: and as she wept, she stooped down, and looked into the sepulchre,
>
> And seeth two angels in white sitting, the one at the head, and the other at the feet, where the body of Jesus had lain.
>
> And they say unto her, Woman, why weepest thou? She saith unto them, Because they have taken away my Lord, and I know not where they have laid him.
>
> And when she had thus said, she turned herself back, and saw Jesus standing, and knew not that it was Jesus.
>
> Jesus saith unto her, Woman, why weepest thou? whom seekest thou? She, supposing him to be the gardener, saith unto him, Sir, if thou have borne him hence, tell me where thou hast laid him, and I will take him away.
>
> Jesus saith unto her, Mary. She turned herself, and saith unto him, Rabboni; which is to say, Master.
>
> Jesus saith unto her, Touch me not; for I am not yet ascended to my Father: but go to my brethren, and say unto

them, I ascend unto my Father, and your Father; and to my God, and your God. (John 20:11–17.)

The Son of God was the firstfruits of the Resurrection. On Easter morning we have a jubilee celebration in honor of Him. Every soul that ever has or will live will follow Him and be resurrected to some state of glory forever and ever. President Benson declared, "No event could be more important to individuals or nations than the resurrection of the Master."

### EASTER'S RESURRECTION

The day grew dark and dreary, the earth a shudder gave.
The temple veil was rent in twain; the elements did rave.
A torn and bruised and battered body hung on a lonely
    cross,
While blood and sweat with holy tears bore witness of the
    loss.
Brutal men with evil thorns bedecked His head with crown.
Crude soldiers bartered for His robe, still others kneeled
    down.
Some friends stood beneath the cross, while others stood
    afar.
The door of death was near at hand, resurrection's door
    ajar.
Evil and vicious men rejoiced; holy men in sorrow bowed.
The Father's Spirit had withdrawn as if behind a shroud.

With vinegar and gall they ministered, nor friends did
    intercede.
They pierced his side with sharpened sword, an ugly final
    deed.
Beyond all pain His body hung; the Son of God was dead.
Disciples wept in silence; His blood was scarlet red.
But rise again He promised, and rise again He did.
All He had been commanded, all His father bid.

Withholding naught, nor pride, nor pain, nor even life was
    spared,
Nor glory did He ever seek, nor was His suffering shared.
The resurrected Christ, the risen Lord, our King of kings
    and God—
For all will follow Him and find the resurrection's path He
    trod.

Christ has risen, hope is renewed, death's grip has lost its
power, and man will live again. Hosanna, hosanna to God and to
the spotless incomparable Savior of the world.

PART TWO

. . .

# OUR MODEL

. . .

## CHAPTER TEN

# His Mercy Endureth Forever

Every Latter-day Saint who has come to know the Master understands fully the statement in James 5:11 "that the Lord is very pitiful, and of tender mercy." In this sense, *pitiful* does not mean "a person or thing deserving of pity," as we tend to think; rather, in the LDS edition of the Bible, the footnote connected to the word *pitiful* directs the reader to the entry "Compassion" in the Topical Guide.

Never was an act of mercy so eternally compassionate as Jesus Christ's atonement and His suffering on the cross. That act of love and mercy was the single most significant extension of mercy—and pity, if you will—in all of eternity. It was absolutely essential to our eternal joy and destiny.

Amulek taught:

> And thus he shall bring salvation to all those who shall believe on his name; this being the intent of this last sacrifice, to bring about the bowels of mercy, which overpowereth justice, and bringeth about means unto men that they may have faith unto repentance.

And thus mercy can satisfy the demands of justice, and encircles them in the arms of safety, while he that exercises no faith unto repentance is exposed to the whole law of the demands of justice. (Alma 34:15–16.)

Amulek was quick to remind us that mercy can satisfy the demands of justice only as we exercise faith unto repentance. In chapter 2 we examined justice according to the supreme goodness of God. I thank God every day of my life for justice. Alma helps us see properly the balance between justice and mercy:

> And now, there was no means to reclaim men from this fallen state, which man had brought upon himself because of his own disobedience;
>
> Therefore, according to justice, the plan of redemption could not be brought about, only on conditions of repentance of men in this probationary state, yea, this preparatory state; for except it were for these conditions, mercy could not take effect except it should destroy the work of justice. Now the work of justice could not be destroyed; if so, God would cease to be God. (Alma 42:12–13.)

Then the prophet declared: "And now, the plan of mercy could not be brought about except an atonement should be made; therefore God himself atoneth for the sins of the world, to bring about the plan of mercy, to appease the demands of justice, that God might be a perfect, just God, and a merciful God also." (Verse 15.)

What a wonderfully merciful blessing the Atonement is! Consider, as Alma stated, that mercy cannot be extended to a person unless that person comes unto Christ. Acceptance of the conditions of the Atonement are personal. The submissive, meek, and obedient who keep the commandments will rejoice in the mercy of our Redeemer.

There is an old epitaph that states:

> Here lies David Elginbrod
> Have mercy on him, God.

As he would do if he were God
And you were David Elginbrod.

We are all exposed to angels of mercy. We see them in all walks of life. A marvelous Relief Society president was having dinner with her family. All of a sudden she jumped up and headed for the door. Her husband asked, "What is this all about?" She said, "I'll tell you later." She was gone in an instant. The husband and family finished eating; they cleaned up the table, put the food away, and did the dishes. About half an hour later, this good woman returned. Her husband asked immediately and with some concern, "What was so urgent?" She explained that she had had the strongest feelings that she needed to go to the bishop's home. When she arrived, she knocked on the door, and the bishop's wife answered. The Relief Society president said simply, "I am here; how can I help?" The bishop's wife burst into tears.

She explained that she had thought about her great husband and how much the people in the ward loved him. They talked with him, called him, thanked him in their testimonies on fast Sunday. She said, "He's wonderful and everybody loves him." Then she wondered about herself. She was not important; no one even knew she was around. She said she even doubted that God knew about her or even cared. She knelt down and prayed, "Heavenly Father, if you know that I exist, or if you even care or know I am here, please let me know." Just then the doorbell rang. When she answered the door, the Relief Society president was there to say, "I am here; how can I help?" They embraced. Through the mercy of a loving God, a sweet bishop's wife received an assurance of His love for her.

Elder J Ballard Washburn is serving as one of the Seventy. Not only is he a General Authority, he is one of the most Christ-like men I have ever met. He is, as someone described, "a man of steel and velvet." He was once a stake president in Page, Arizona. His stake included part of the Indian reservation. His counselor in the stake presidency was his home teaching companion, at least during one memorable experience that this counselor shared with me. He and President Washburn went into a hogan. There they found three children alone. The mother and father had not been home for two or three days, apparently on a drinking binge. As I recall, there was an eight-year-old boy, a five-year-old girl, and a two-year-old boy. The hogan was messy and the stench terrible. The two-year-old had a diaper on that hadn't been changed in three days. The excrement had caked and dried on his bottom, leaving it clearly irritated and possibly infected.

The counselor related, "I stayed in the hogan as long as I could stand it, then I had to leave." He went outside and took several deep breaths of fresh air. Then he waited and waited. President Washburn did not come out of the hogan, so his counselor went back in. President Washburn had sent the eight-year-old for a basin of water. He carefully removed the baby's diaper and then soaked the dried excrement until it could be softened; then he tenderly removed it. He cleaned up the little boy's bottom and gently dried it. He sent the brother for another towel. When he returned, Elder Washburn pinned the towel on in place of the diaper, and then he picked the Indian boy up in his arms and loved and kissed him. What a sweet and merciful thing to do! There are many opportunities for each of us to extend mercy to someone in need.

In this light, James Kavanaugh composed an interesting poem entitled "Will You Be My Friend?"

### WILL YOU BE MY FRIEND?

Will you be my friend?
There are so many reasons why you never should:
I'm sometimes sullen, often shy, acutely sensitive.
My fear erupts as anger, I find it hard to give.
I talk about myself when I'm afraid
And often spend a day without anything to say.
    But I will make you laugh
    And love you quite a bit
    And hold you when you're sad.

## His Mercy Endureth Forever

I cry a little almost every day
Because I'm more caring than the strangers ever know.
And, if at times, I show my tender side
(The soft and warmer part I hide)
 I wonder,
 Will you be my friend?
A friend
 Who far beyond the feebleness of any vow or tie
 Will touch the secret place where I am really I.
 To know the pain of lips that plead and eyes that weep,
 Who will not run away when you find me in the street
 Alone and lying mangled by my quota of defeats
 But will stop and stay—to tell me of another day
 When I was beautiful.

Will you be my friend?
There are so many reasons why you never should:
Often I'm too serious, seldom predictably the same,
Sometimes cold and distant, probably I'll always change.
I bluster and brag, seek attention like a child,
I brood and pout, my anger can be wild.
 But I will make you laugh
 And love you quite a bit
 And be near when you're afraid.
I shake a little almost every day
Because I'm more frightened than the strangers ever know
And if at times I show my trembling side
(The anxious, fearful part I hide)
 I wonder,
 Will you be my friend?
A friend
 Who, when I fear your closeness, feels me push away
 And stubbornly will stay to share what's left on such a day,
 Who, when no one knows my name or calls me on the
  phone,

When there's no concern for me—what I have or haven't
   done—
And those I've helped and counted on have, oh so deftly,
   run,
Who, when there's nothing left but me, stripped of
   charm and subtlety,
Will nonetheless remain.

Will you be my friend?
   For no reason that I know
   Except I want you so.

I have a wonderful friend named Margie Harward, from
Salina, Utah. Years ago she came to my office for a special blessing
and has kept in touch since then. Although she is a wonderful, loving, kind friend to many people, life has not been kind to her. She
has suffered greatly all her adult life. It seems as though she barely
gets through one serious health problem when another immediately besets her.

I have learned that Margie is far more concerned about others
than she is about herself. She has blessed the lives of a multitude of
people, often when she herself is not well. In her exuberance to lift
others' loads, she rarely thinks of herself. When she dies, it will
probably be from a broken heart—she hurts intensely when others
suffer. Her tender, sensitive, and merciful heart is obvious. I have
confidence that the Lord, in His great mercy, will cradle and watch
over her and compensate her for every moment of her own personal suffering. Has he not taught, "Blessed are the merciful: for
they shall obtain mercy"? (Matthew 5:7.)

Quite often as we read about mercy, we think of love, charity,
kindness, and understanding. There are few places where we come
to understand this better than in the hymn "How Firm a
Foundation." Review the last four verses with me:

When through the deep waters I call thee to go,
The rivers of sorrow shall not thee o'erflow,

For I will be with thee, thy troubles to bless,
And sanctify to thee thy deepest distress.

When through fiery trials thy pathway shall lie,
My grace, all sufficient, shall be thy supply.
The flame shall not hurt thee; I only design
Thy dross to consume and thy gold to refine.

E'en down to old age, all my people shall prove
My sov'reign, eternal, unchangeable love;
And then, when gray hair shall their temples adorn,
Like lambs shall they still in my bosom be borne.

The soul that on Jesus hath leaned for repose
I will not, I cannot, desert to his foes;
That soul, though all hell should endeavor to shake,
I'll never, no never, no never forsake!

(*HYMNS*, NO. 85.)

I believe those beautiful lyrics reflect the feelings and love of the Savior. In another place we see the depth of the Savior's mercy:

And it came to pass that when Jesus had thus spoken, he cast his eyes round about again on the multitude, and beheld they were in tears, and did look steadfastly upon him as if they would ask him to tarry a little longer with them.

And he said unto them: Behold, my bowels are filled with compassion towards you.

Have ye any that are sick among you? Bring them hither. Have ye any that are lame, or blind, or halt, or maimed, or leprous, or that are withered, or that are deaf, or that are afflicted in any manner? Bring them hither and I will heal them, for I have compassion upon you; *my bowels are filled with mercy.* (3 Nephi 17:5–7; emphasis added.)

I find this phrase, "my bowels are filled with mercy," to be fraught with power and beauty. Mercy and compassion come from the heart and are born deep inside us. Because of His mercy, as verses 9–10 of this same chapter state,

> when he had thus spoken, all the multitude, with one accord, did go forth with their sick and their afflicted, and their lame, and with their blind, and with their dumb, and with all them that were afflicted in any manner; and he did heal them every one as they were brought forth unto him.
>
> And they did all, both they who had been healed and they who were whole, bow down at his feet, and did worship him; and as many as could come for the multitude did kiss his feet, insomuch that they did bathe his feet with their tears.

Mercy takes away our inhibitions. Those who were healed and those who brought them forth impulsively kissed the Master's feet. J Ballard Washburn changed a humble Indian boy's diaper. The promise is sure and true: "Blessed are the merciful: for they shall obtain mercy." (Matthew 5:7.)

Although mercy cannot take away our pain and our grief, nor can it always remove trials from our path, it is always there to soften, modify, and suffer with us. Many of us would gladly suffer pain personally rather than see a loved one go through it. Fortunately, the Lord does not grant us the request to transfer another's pain and grief to ourselves, regardless of how feverishly we plead. On the other hand, though we are not able to lift totally another's burden—nor should we—sometimes sharing that burden does bring a sweet, spiritual, partial relief to those who are being tried desperately and who are suffering exquisitely. Many find it easier to get through trials when they know that they are not alone and that others they know would be willing to take upon themselves all their pain, if it were possible.

Elder Orson F. Whitney stated: "No pain that we suffer, no trial that we experience is wasted. It ministers to our education, to the development of such qualities as patience, faith, fortitude and humility. All that we suffer and all that we endure, especially when we endure it patiently, builds up our characters, purifies our hearts, expands our souls, and makes us more tender and charitable, more worthy to be called the children of God . . . and it is through sorrow and suffering, toil and tribulation, that we gain the education that we come here to acquire and which will make us more like our Father and Mother in heaven." (Dennis D. Flake, "Orson F. Whitney's Philosophy of Education," p. 96.)

God would not be merciful if He deprived us of the painful and sorrowful experiences of life. Mercy must hold itself in check sometimes and watch from a distance so that those who suffer may grow. The great Elohim in His wonderful mercy watched from a distance while His Only Begotten, Beloved Son suffered in Gethsemane and was hung cruelly on a cross. The mercy that God the Father must have shown after His Son's death on the cross is incomprehensible to the most spiritual of us.

The Savior said to Mary, "Touch me not; for I am not yet ascended to my Father." (John 20:17.) He then went to His Father, the great God Elohim. What sweetness, what pleasure, what exquisite, supernal joy! How could man or woman conceive of the tender, beautiful experience as Son returned to Father and reported that the most difficult task in time or in eternity by man or God had been completed? Imagine the Father taking His Son to His bosom while speaking the words, "This is my beloved Son, in whom I am well pleased." Only the merciful can begin to comprehend such a glorious experience.

King Benjamin, I believe, gave the second greatest recorded discourse in the history of man. The Sermon on the Mount, of course, is the greatest. King Benjamin spoke with such spiritual power that the people "had viewed themselves in their own carnal state, even less than the dust of the earth. And they all cried aloud with one voice, saying: O have mercy, and apply the atoning blood of Christ that we may receive forgiveness of our sins, and our hearts may be purified; for we believe in Jesus Christ, the Son of God, who created heaven and earth, and all things; who shall come down among the children of men." (Mosiah 4:2.)

"Have mercy," they declared, "that we may receive forgiveness of our sins." The process of applying mercy in order to receive a forgiveness of our sins ties directly to the Atonement. Without the Atonement, mercy could not be extended in a way that could bring about the satisfying of the demands of justice. As the people began to understand and feel that God would grant them mercy, King Benjamin said:

> I say unto you, if ye have come to a knowledge of the goodness of God, and his matchless power, and his wisdom, and his patience, and his long-suffering towards the children of men; and also, the atonement which has been prepared from the foundation of the world, that thereby salvation might come to him that should put his trust in the Lord, and should be diligent in keeping his commandments, and continue in the faith even unto the end of his life, I mean the life of the mortal body—
>
> I say, that this is the man who receiveth salvation, through the atonement which was prepared from the foundation of the world for all mankind, which ever were since the fall of Adam, or who are, or who ever shall be, even unto the end of the world.
>
> And this is the means whereby salvation cometh. And there is none other salvation save this which hath been spoken of; neither are there any conditions whereby man can be saved except the conditions which I have told you. (Mosiah 4:6–8.)

The conditions are clear: repentance with a broken heart and a contrite spirit.

Once the people had felt the mercy of Christ and understood how it was extended to each of them, then King Benjamin taught them—and us—all a great and true principle of mercy:

> And also, ye yourselves will succor those that stand in need of your succor; ye will administer of your substance unto him that standeth in need; and ye will not suffer that

the beggar putteth up his petition to you in vain, and turn him out to perish.

Perhaps thou shalt say: The man has brought upon himself his misery; therefore I will stay my hand, and will not give unto him of my food, nor impart unto him of my substance that he may not suffer, for his punishments are just—

But I say unto you, O man, whosoever doeth this the same hath great cause to repent; and except he repenteth of that which he hath done he perisheth forever, and hath no interest in the kingdom of God.

For behold, are we not all beggars? Do we not all depend upon the same Being, even God, for all the substance which we have, for both food and raiment, and for gold, and for silver, and for all the riches which we have of every kind?

And behold, even at this time, ye have been calling on his name, and begging for a remission of your sins. And has he suffered that ye have begged in vain? Nay; he has poured out his Spirit upon you, and has caused that your hearts should be filled with joy, and has caused that your mouths should be stopped that ye could not find utterance, so exceedingly great was your joy.

And now, if God, who has created you, on whom you are dependent for your lives and for all that ye have and are, doth grant unto you whatsoever ye ask that is right, in faith, believing that ye shall receive, O then, how ye ought to impart of the substance that ye have one to another. (Mosiah 4:16–21.)

Verse 20 refers to the exceedingly great joy that came to them after they felt mercy. Mercy is a heartfelt emotion. It comes from deep within us. The Savior's reference to His bowels being filled with mercy is significant. When we feel mercy for someone, we don't get a headache; we hurt inside.

Emotions are felt in the breast, not the head. Peace and a burning in the bosom are heartfelt emotions. The merciful always have Christ-like feelings and emotions as they witness the hurt, sorrows, and heartaches of others. The Savior exemplified His own teachings as He extended His mercy to the woman taken in adultery, the widow of Nain, the man with palsy, and so many others.

We must always remember the Lord's promise, "Blessed are the merciful: for they shall obtain mercy." Our salvation is at least somewhat dependent on this principle. Mercy is a divine gift. If we would be merciful, we must act as Christ would act. In addition to keeping the Ten Commandments, we must obey the eleventh commandment, which is His "new commandment": "As I have loved you, . . . love one another." (John 13:34.)

May we all become possessors and givers of mercy to those around us; if we will do so, we will in turn "obtain mercy" ourselves from Him whose right it is to give.

## CHAPTER ELEVEN

# Charity Is Greater Than Faith

"A nd now abideth faith, hope, charity, these three; but the greatest of these is charity." (1 Corinthians 13:13.) If Paul is correct, and I believe he is, then charity is greater than faith. That is
quite a declaration when we consider what can be accomplished
by faith. Those who have sufficient faith—such as the brother of
Jared and Joseph Smith—can part the veil. Those who have faith
can move mountains, rebuke the storms, control the elements,
divide the waters, and turn rivers upstream. Through faith the
blind are able to see, the deaf have their ears opened and can hear,
the dead are raised, and the diseased are healed; and through faith
the transgressor may be cleansed every whit.

Ammon declared that it was by faith that thousands were
brought to the redeeming love of the Master. (Alma 26:22.)

Abraham Maslow claimed that self-actualization is the pinnacle of motivations. The scriptures and modern prophets, however, make it clear that faith in Christ is greater. How is it, then,
that charity could be greater than faith? In the thirteenth chapter
of 1 Corinthians, Paul describes what those with faith may

accomplish and still not possess charity. Through faith we can speak with the tongues of men and of angels. We can have the gift of prophecy, bestow our goods to the poor, give our bodies to be burned—and still not possess charity. We can have the ministering of angels and see visions. Can charity be greater than all of these? Indeed it is. Charity is the very essence of the gospel of Jesus Christ. It is the very conduct and total being of the Savior. Charity is the pure love of Christ. Those who have charity are directed by it in everything they do. It becomes the central motivation for their living and being.

All who would be disciples of Christ desire to possess the gift of charity. As I have wrestled over the years with what charity is, I have always come up short. As I now grow older, I think I am gaining some slight additional insight. It cannot be explained in words, only in deeds. Let me share a few examples.

A Relief Society president of whom I am aware awakened her husband and family at 2:30 A.M. so they could go to the temple to be sealed. They arrived at the temple early in the morning for an appointment with the mission president to sign their temple recommends. The mission president must have forgotten the appointment. The family waited at the temple. All morning they waited; then all afternoon. Someone must have asked them for whom they were waiting. Just before the second to last session of the day began, the mission president came, interviewed them, and signed their recommends. They quietly went into the temple, received their endowments, and were sealed as a family. Not one negative word or judgment came from their mouths. They thought only of the great joy and excitement that came from being sealed as a family for eternity.

Charity is not finding fault, even when you are offended. Charity includes keeping the objective of your life—such as the family above who focused on being sealed—predominant over all other frustrations and considerations.

Charity also includes your attitude toward those who have not. In all of my reading, I cannot recall one experience of the

Savior asking a man whether he was working, whether he would have worked if he had a job, or even whether he was worthy to receive charity. He seemed to never have a concern about inappropriate begging. Consider the palsied man who was lowered through the roof, the two blind men calling to Him during His triumphal entry to Jerusalem, or the Canaanite woman. When He fed the five thousand and the seven thousand, He did not ask how many had personal supplies or who had eaten most recently; he gave freely to all. Sometimes when we are accosted by panhandlers, beggars, or the poor, we have excuses why we will not give. These excuses are often legitimate. The recipient might be going right back into a bar or liquor store; he or she might indeed be part of a syndicate; a woman might be carrying another's infant or child merely to evoke sympathy. Maybe the emergency for which they need financial help is fabricated. But then again, *maybe not*. What if we truly turn away the needy? If we give to the poor and the panhandler, the beggar and the widow—deserving or undeserving—it will be accounted unto us as righteousness. Charity, in my humble opinion, would suggest that it does not make any difference. In fact, I believe that those who best exemplify charity do not think about worthiness; they simply give.

Elder Collado, our regional representative in the Philippines, said about one man, "He has the quickest draw in the West when it comes to reaching for his wallet to give to the poor." Could we ever be justifiably accused of having such a quick draw?

The widow contributing her mite to the treasury represented charity. She knew that the treasury was just that—the treasury of the synagogue—and that many contributed in a great or ordinary way. The Lord truly did not need her mite, but He got it. She simply cast in her all.

Charity is a motivating force so powerful that it overrides all selfishness, vanity, false pity, arrogance, pride, deceit, and desire for praise. "Charity never faileth." As we begin to understand charity, we find that it affects all that we do.

Sometimes charity gives the appearance of indulgence. For

example, sometimes General Authorities encounter situations such as the following: Leaders of a stake far from Salt Lake City spend days, even weeks, in preparation for a visiting authority; he arrives and is revered as God's servant. Everyone wants him to be as comfortable and cared for as possible. A nice room has been reserved at a hotel, and special dinners have been arranged. How would those leaders feel if the authority arrived and promptly said, "This is too nice a room; put me in a simple one, please." And then what if he were to cancel a dinner that had been in preparation for several days so he could go to his room and save his hosts the trouble of dinner. Sometimes we bless the lives of marvelous, sweet, simple souls by accepting with gratitude what they have done. Remember that when the woman washed the Savior's feet and began to anoint them with *costly* oil, the Savior did not forbid her.

Sometimes we as General Authorities, if we are to show true charity, must simply let the Saints receive the deep and wonderful pleasure they feel from serving those who have been called as the Lord's ministers to the world. To do otherwise might be more of an affront to the Lord and the Saints, who have such great love for the Lord's servants. We all know that we are on the Lord's errand. We know that the Lord, not us as individuals, is the focus of attention and affection when people make such great preparations.

Each of us has likely been criticized unjustly at least once. Furthermore, sometimes other people take the credit for our work or success. Often we are misjudged for our motives. Some take offense when we intend none. A few may judge us inaccurately or misunderstand our attitude. To all of these, the person who truly has charity is forgiving. He or she simply knows that the person finding fault may be in some way pleading for help. It may be a lack of self-esteem, a constant measuring of oneself against everyone else and forever falling short, or a similar lack of achievement or success. Charity would dictate that we try to see all that is good and holy and light in the offending one, and then return good for evil.

Is it truly possible to understand charity? I have thought much about this. I now believe that this is an impossible task, but with the help of the Savior, who is the author and distributor of charity, we may increase our understanding. Charity must be an absolute and total submission of mind and heart in a completely selfless way so that we can serve every other human soul with the purest of motives. We cannot expect appreciation, gratitude, or any kind of reward except the natural consequences of blessing another's life.

Vanity would prevent all but the pure in heart from the above attitude. In his epistle to Titus, Paul stated, "Unto the pure all things are pure." (Titus 1:15.) Purity ties directly to charity. All of my life these two—charity and purity—have been a compelling mental crusade. I have written several books—three of them are *Charity Never Faileth, Purity of Heart,* and *More Purity Give Me*—and still a full understanding and comprehension eludes me. I try in vain to write "the smallest part" of what I feel about charity and purity. My personal quest since I was a young man was to strive to have absolute charity and be completely pure. As I sat down to write this time, I thought my effort might be more fruitful, but again I fall short in defining charity. However, I do know when I see it, for I see examples every day, usually manifest in small or seemingly insignificant experiences.

Charity gets no pleasure out of humiliation, embarrassment, jealousy, revenge, undeserved praise, or unearned titles or positions. We all encounter embarrassment at some time or another, whether it be inadvertently tipping over a glass at dinnertime or getting to the checkstand with more groceries than money. Grateful I am that I have seen and known of several of the latter instances happening, and in each case someone who was waiting reached hurriedly into his wallet and made up the deficit. I can think of little that exemplifies spontaneous charity as well as such moments.

"Charity suffereth long, and is kind." (1 Corinthians 13:4.) Every member of the Church would do well to be kind. The more kindly people are, the nearer they come to charity. The *American*

*College Dictionary* makes this statement about the word *kind:* "*Kind* implies a deep-seated characteristic shown either habitually or on occasion by considerate behavior." A kind person is good and has a benevolent nature and disposition. If we would possess charity, we would be kind.

Lest any misunderstand, we can all have a great deal of faith—as Paul suggested in 1 Corinthians 13—and perform great miracles and do many wonderful things and not yet possess charity. However, there are those who speak with tongues of men and angels and do have charity. It has been my experience that those who have great knowledge, who possess faith to move mountains, who bestow their goods to feed the poor, and who will walk unhesitatingly into the jaws of hell if necessary to save a soul almost always possess charity.

The following teachings from the Master best represent charity to me. They help us understand the full dimension of Christ's life:

- "Neither do I condemn thee: go, and sin no more." (John 8:11.)
- "Blessed are the poor in spirit . . . [and] they that mourn." (Matthew 5:3–4.)
- "Blessed are the meek . . . [and] they which do hunger and thirst after righteousness." (Matthew 5:5–6.)
- "Blessed are the merciful, . . . the pure in heart, . . . the peacemakers." (Matthew 5:7–9.)
- "Inasmuch as ye have done it unto one of the least of these my brethren, ye have done it unto me." (Matthew 25:40.)
- "Peace be unto thy soul." (D&C 121:7.)
- "Come unto me, all ye that labour and are heavy laden, and I will give you rest." (Matthew 11:28.)
- "And now the year of my redeemed is come; and they shall mention the loving kindness of their Lord, and all that he has bestowed upon them according to his goodness, and according to his loving kindness, forever and ever." (D&C 133:52.)
- "And God shall wipe away all tears from their eyes; and there

shall be no more death, neither sorrow, nor crying, neither shall there be any more pain." (Revelation 21:4.)

• "Greater love hath no man than this, that a man lay down his life for his friends. Ye are my friends." (John 15:13–14.)

• "Though your sins be as scarlet, they shall be as white as snow; though they be red like crimson, they shall be as wool." (Isaiah 1:18.)

• "If I will not open you the windows of heaven, and pour you out a blessing, that there shall not be room enough to receive it." (Malachi 3:10.)

• "Forgive them; for they know not what they do." (Luke 23:34.)

• "Wherefore, Father, spare these my brethren that believe on my name, that they may come unto me and have everlasting life." (D&C 45:5.)

• Look unto me, and endure to the end, and ye shall live." (3 Nephi 15:9.)

• "And no one can conceive of the joy which filled our souls at the time we heard him pray for us unto the Father." (3 Nephi 17:17.)

• "And when he had said these words, he wept." (3 Nephi 17:21.)

We could continue with an endless list of scriptures that reflect the Savior's charity. Jesus taught much, but the supreme virtue of charity He especially exemplified. He is the one perfect model of all righteousness and charity.

Paul taught, "Now we see through a glass, darkly; but then face to face: now I know in part, but then shall I know even as also I am known." (1 Corinthians 13:12.) What a blessing it will be in the eternal world to know each person's heart and mind and for them in turn to know our very thoughts and reasons. We will be like transparent crystal. We will know the deepest motivation, the unspoken words, even those thoughts we do not have the ability to communicate. Imagine the day that will come when all of the beautiful unspoken phrases, words, and utterances that should have been spoken will all be understood.

The greatest and most blessed character virtue in all of humanity is charity. It is the main fabric through which all other virtues weave to make a perfect tapestry of life. However, in order to possess charity, we must be pure in heart, chaste, and filled with faith; we must abide in hope, serve spontaneously with love, lift, bless, obey, wear out our lives in service, respond, give to the poor, bless the widow and orphan, clothe the naked, feed the hungry, judge not, seek not for glory or praise, forgive without reservation, and love with all of our hearts—only then do we begin to approach charity. Remember, "charity never faileth"—not ever.

And ultimately, if we are possessors of charity, we will be possessed by Him who is the author of charity.

CHAPTER TWELVE

. . .

# Leaders Tread with Courage
# Where Christ Would Have Us Tread

In chapter 54 of Alma, Captain Moroni negotiated with Ammoron for an exchange of prisoners. Because the Nephites did not take women and children as prisoners, Moroni demanded an exchange only on the basis that a Nephite prisoner, his wife, and his children be traded for one Lamanite prisoner.

Ammoron, the leader of the Lamanites, agreed to this only because it would preserve his food. However, Moroni also made another demand as a prerequisite to exchanging prisoners, a demand that Ammoron would not meet. That demand was that Ammoron would withdraw from his wicked purposes.

In verses 12–14, Captain Moroni's "treatise" to Ammoron states:

> If ye do not this, I will come against you with my armies;
> yea, even I will arm my women and my children, and I will
> come against you, and I will follow you even into your own
> land, which is the land of our first inheritance; yea, and it
> shall be blood for blood, yea, life for life; and I will give you

battle even until you are destroyed from off the face of the earth.

Behold, I am in my anger, and also my people; ye have sought to murder us, and we have only sought to defend ourselves. But behold, if ye seek to destroy us more we will seek to destroy you; yea, and we will seek our land, the land of our first inheritance.

Now I close my epistle. I am Moroni; *I am a leader.* (Emphasis added.)

In my copy of the Book of Mormon I have written in the margin, "Never have truer words been spoken than when Moroni declared, 'I am a leader.'" What a leader!

Many years later, Moroni was described in these words: "If all men had been, and were, and ever would be, like unto Moroni, behold, the very powers of hell would have been shaken forever; yea, the devil would never have power over the hearts of the children of men." (Alma 48:17.)

When Moroni was chief commander over the Nephite armies:

He rent his coat; and he took a piece thereof, and wrote upon it—In memory of our God, our religion, and freedom, and our peace, our wives, and our children—and he fastened it upon the end of a pole.

And he fastened on his headplate, and his breastplate, and his shields, and girded on his armor about his loins; and he took the pole, which had on the end thereof his rent coat, (and he called it the title of liberty) and he bowed himself to the earth, and he prayed mightily unto his God for the blessings of liberty to rest upon his brethren, so long as there should a band of Christians remain to possess the land. (Alma 46:12–13.)

There was no question in Moroni's mind that he was a leader. He knew his role, and he intended to fulfill it. He lined up in the right direction with his whole soul. He put his faith to work by action and by kneeling in prayer, and he wasn't ashamed to do either publicly.

Moroni was an undaunted leader with an unconquerable spirit. His heart and soul were in a cause greater than himself; he felt not one particle of fear. Whenever I read about Captain Moroni, a fire burns in the very marrow of my bones. What would you give to fight side by side with a man such as this?

Men, women, and youth will always rally to a cause when they have a leader; however, it is difficult for God or any organization to use a reluctant leader.

Take note of how Captain Moroni led. First, he set a standard and called it "Title of Liberty." It included the things that matter most: "our God and our freedom, our wives and our children." Then he enlisted the help of the Almighty God of heaven. He asked that the powers of heaven would rest upon him and his people as long as there remained a "band of Christians to possess the land." (Alma 46:13.)

No wonder that men such as Helaman, Teancum, Lehi, and others rallied to the cause. A leader of Captain Moroni's stature has a plan, makes a commitment, and then—with his total will and the help of God—marches forth into battle. It is also interesting that he had to "clean house" among the Nephites before he moved against the Lamanites. A leader knows that unity in a cause is essential. Internal rot and disease must be removed before an army moves forth to do battle with the enemy.

I am certain that Moroni did not really know how great he was. I doubt that he ever studied a leadership principle from a popular book or costly seminar. There simply came a great need, and Moroni, in his purity and confidence, stepped forward and allowed the Lord to use him.

In the Church, we are all leaders and followers. The Church is so organized that even the least among us leads during his or her life. This leadership might take the form of a few families to home teach, or it might be a stake, region, or even an area calling; it may be a class of Young Women, or it may be all the young women in the Church.

Because we must all face leadership, I would like to focus on the foundation pillars for gospel leaders who would follow Christ.

President Harold B. Lee suggested that only as we make ourselves totally available can we become worthy disciples of Christ. Interestingly, lack of self-confidence or feelings of unworthiness do not conflict with this thought. Moses and Enoch both were "slow of speech" and wondered at the call. We may feel inadequate, but when there is a job to do, someone needs to step forward and do it.

The fourth section of the Doctrine and Covenants states, "If ye have desires to serve God ye are called to the work." (Verse 3.) Quite often we get confused semantically by this phrase. To a servant of God, leadership means service. In the Lord's affairs, His great leaders are those who are servants of all. The Master Himself performed the greatest act in time or in eternity. The act was so profound and terrible to contemplate that even He shrunk "and would that [He] might not drink the bitter cup." His leadership as a servant and His absolute obedience to His Father took him along dark, bitter paths. He described His suffering as "sore," "exquisite," and "hard to bear"; it caused Him to tremble because of the pain and to bleed at every pore. (D&C 19:18.) Jesus said, "I have overcome and have trodden the winepress alone, even the winepress of the fierceness of the wrath of the Almighty God." (D&C 76:107.) He knew that there was no other way, nor had there ever been— nor would there ever be on this earth—any other soul who could satisfy the demands of justice.

The necessity of an atonement was part of God's eternal plan of salvation and exaltation. God's program provided the eternal laws and also the obedience that would bring consequential blessings. Their violation would bring down the strong hand of justice. There is always a consequence when we violate the laws of God through disobedience or inaction (sins of omission). It is an eternal principle that justice must be satisfied. Justice is a great benefactor to the righteous but a terrible taskmaster to those who transgress. It is a wonderful relief to those who suffer for righteousness' sake through illness, death, divorce, handicap, or affliction. We will suffer no trial in this life that the Savior has not experienced vicariously. That is why the Savior counseled, "Listen to him who is the advocate with the Father, who is pleading your cause before him—Saying: Father, behold the sufferings and death of him who did no sin, in whom thou wast well pleased; behold the blood of thy Son which was shed, the blood of him whom thou gavest that thyself might be glorified." (D&C 45:3–4.)

You will note that *sufferings* is plural in His prayer. He can and will be the advocate for all those who suffer or who transgress and truly repent. What greater role could a true servant-leader play in all of eternity?

A righteous leader who makes himself or herself available will accomplish great and noble things. I remember talking to Elder Mechalek, a stake president and then regional representative in Argentina. His brother also served as a high councilor and as a stake president. When they were boys, they overheard the missionaries who had baptized them talking about their missions. One of the missionaries said, "Is it really worth it? We have spent thirty months in Argentina. It has required a lot of money to support us." They could have added that they had put off their schooling and marriage and worked hard. The only success they had was baptizing the Mechalek brothers. Was it worth it?

Both of the brothers grew up and went on missions in South American countries. Both of them baptized over a hundred converts. Many of their converts have now been on missions, and some of those have baptized hundreds. Now some of *their* converts have been on missions and baptized great numbers. Someone said, "You can count the seeds in an apple, but you cannot count the apples in a seed." Who knows what the eventual numbers may be?

The two missionaries performed a wondrous work by simply making themselves available. Was it worth it? Unquestionably! Ted Olsen said:

And ninety and nine are with dreams content,
but the hope of a world made new
Is the hundredth man who is grimly bent
on making the dream come true.

All who make themselves available and have willing hearts will be called to lead. It is part of the gospel plan.

We have been privileged to live in an interesting time in the history of the world. Tremendous things are taking place. Richard Kostsya, in a talk in British Columbia on 1 May 1990, made the following observations:

> The real beginning of a direct-broadcast satellite [DBS] era in the United States was announced earlier this year. N.B.C. Cablevision, Murdock's new corporation, and Hughes Communication have pooled $1 billion to launch sky cable . . . a system that will employ high-powered satellites to beam 108 channels to households all over America. This time the DBS receiving dishes will be widely affordable—only $200 to $300. It is 12 inches across and can be inconspicuously installed on walls or window ledges.
>
> Previous efforts to launch DBS services were costly failures . . . but those failures are similar to early attempts to build a workable airplane . . . they're the trials and errors necessary to build a successful machine. . . .
>
> DBS could completely obviate need for cable systems and television stations. I couldn't begin to contemplate the kind of changes our industry would undergo at that point. (*Vital Speeches*, October 1990, p. 22.)

Later in his talk he suggested that the television itself will become something quite different in the not-too-distant future as the simple TV set is replaced by a video communications center.

Such is the vision one man has for television and the media communications field. As overwhelming as that vision might seem, it is relatively insignificant when compared to the great, eternal vision our modern prophets have for this church and its members. I bear a witness borne of experience that when a General Authority receives the mantle of his calling, he has additional vision and insight.

When I served as general president of the Young Men, I could almost hear a clarion call to the young men of the Church. I could see them coming in bands of thousands and tens of thousands to fulfill their sacred callings in the Aaronic Priesthood. I had a feeling everywhere I went, every time I spoke, that there were young men and young women in the congregation who would do magnificent and marvelous things. I often wondered whether the young man that would be the prophet of the Church thirty or forty or fifty years from now was in the congregation. I wondered if there were young men in those meetings who would sit among the Twelve or the Seventy. I always tried to teach well and warn these and all future leaders to stay clean and sweet and pure.

A leader must be able to have a vision of the work. President Spencer W. Kimball, at the April 1974 regional representatives training seminar, gave such a powerful vision of missionary work that I leaned over to Elder H. Burke Peterson and said, "I believe President Kimball has had a personal priesthood interview with the Savior." Whether that was the case, I have no way of knowing, but I do believe that President Kimball could envision a great flood of missionaries covering the earth. Within two years we had almost doubled the number of missionaries in the field—that was only the beginning of his vision.

President Ezra Taft Benson had a vision of the destiny of the Book of Mormon ministry. The first time I heard him talk about his vision of the Book of Mormon, I thought his whole statement should be included in the Doctrine and Covenants.

I once heard President Howard W. Hunter speak of a holy hand that is involved in this work. If ever anyone on the face of the earth represented the sweet, gentle, kind, wonderful traits of Jesus, it was Howard W. Hunter. I felt a vision of the love the Master must have for us as I observed President Hunter. The Saints referred to Elder LeGrand Richards as their "Beloved Apostle," and indeed he was. I believe in time they will refer to President Howard W. Hunter as the "Apostle of Love."

President Gordon B. Hinckley has had a unique ministry in the Church. He has served as counselor to three prophets in this dispensation. President Kimball, President Benson, and President Hunter were able to function only in a limited way during the latter part of their ministry. Much of the weight of responsibility carried by the First Presidency has rested on President Hinckley's capable shoulders. He has dedicated over half of the temples built in this dispensation. He has carefully monitored the finances and building program of the Church. He has a special understanding and vision of the individual members of the Church. He has a vision of the image that the Church must eventually present to the world—a Church dressed in its beautiful garments. He gave a talk at the University of Utah, giving a vision of interfaith unity and the value of the Church in the Utah community. He did so in a spiritually brilliant way, giving no offense. His masterful discourse has helped improve the image of the Church. I believe President Hinckley has a vision of the Church becoming fair as the sun and clear as the moon.

President Thomas S. Monson is a marvel. He has a remarkable vision of the Master's true ministry—welfare as the essence of the gospel. President Monson understands not only the welfare programs as few do in the Church today, but he also understands the Master's ministry of compassion for the poor, the widow, the orphan, the suffering. He is a gentle spiritual giant. He is a man for all seasons. President Monson has a brilliant mind with memory capabilities that could come only through an endowment from God. All who have ever known him or met him have a feeling that he is their personal friend. President Monson's vision of this great latter-day work comes from his vast experience and his tremendous leadership capabilities. He is the kind of a leader for whom people gladly put their total heart and soul into the work.

We have recently sustained President James E. Faust, this

gentle giant of the Lord. His wisdom and judgment are constant. He has an understanding of the principle of righteousness. He is selfless in all his service. What a marvelous work he will accomplish! His legal background and his lifetime of Church leadership have prepared him for this very hour. He is a holy servant of God. He is thoughtful and concerned about the women and children of this church.

"Where there is no vision, the people perish," but they also do not perform. (Proverbs 29:18.) They have no heart for the work and will inevitably impair rather than assist. Similarly, a leader with no vision will dramatically limit his effectiveness.

Habbakuk had a vision of the work. "Behold," said he, "ye among the heathen, and regard, and wonder marvelously: for I will work a work in your days, which ye will not believe, though it be told you." (Habbakuk 1:5.)

If vision is so important, how do we gain it? Those who have vision have many things in common:

- They see the total work before them.
- They visualize what must happen in order to get the results they desire.
- They consider all of their resources, potentials, and capabilities collectively.
- They see in their mind what marvelous and magnificent things could happen when the total work force is mobilized unitedly.
- They then go to work to accomplish their goal.
- They have the ability to communicate their vision to those around them in a convincing way so that others are enlisted also.
- They see what they are doing as a cause, not a project.
- Religious leaders feel a "holy hand" assisting in the work.

President Kimball had a vision that we would need to put forth a tremendous effort to prepare native missionaries for the day when foreign missionaries would not be permitted to enter those countries. Already this has taken place in several countries, and the proselyting work continues because of the vision of one holy man.

In the most simple way, a Sunday School teacher can have a vision of every one of his or her class members growing up in faith and going to the temple. People must also have a vision of their own personal lives—a humble, sweet belief that God intended us to do something larger and greater.

President Joseph F. Smith said:

> After we have done all we could do for the cause of truth, and withstood the evil that men have brought upon us, and we have been overwhelmed by their wrongs, it is still our duty to stand. We cannot give up; we must not lie down. Great causes are not won in a single generation. To stand firm in the face of overwhelming opposition, when you have done all you can, is the courage of faith. The courage of faith is the courage of progress. Men who possess that divine quality go on; they are not permitted to stand still if they would. They are not simply the creatures of their own power and wisdom; they are instrumentalities of a higher law and a divine purpose. (*Gospel Doctrine* [Salt Lake City: Deseret Book Co., 1939], p. 119.)

Imagine with me the magnitude of the cause in which we are engaged. We have been given the keys, the priesthood, and the program for the greatest cause in eternity. We alone of all God's children have the keys of knowledge of salvation and exaltation. All the myriad souls who ever have or do now or will walk the earth must be taught the gospel of Jesus Christ. They must, if they desire exaltation and are accountable, accept that gospel and be baptized into His only true Church. This Church alone holds the keys of sealing husbands and wives and their children together as families for all eternity.

The cause is greater than men or prophets. It is the cause of the Savior. It is the cause of God the Eternal Father. By enlisting in His cause and faithfully enduring, we will be the recipients of all we are teaching and sharing. A verse we quote so often, sometimes without much thought, is "This is my work and my glory—to bring to pass the immortality and eternal life of man." (Moses 1:39.) Imagine a cause with eternal implications and consequences, a cause so great that all eternity hangs in the balance as we accept or reject it. We do not fully comprehend what a magnificent privilege it is to be fully enlisted.

This one great cause has a thousand and one—or more—subsidiary causes. We can each be part of at least one of these great causes.

When I walked down the jetway in San Antonio, Texas, as a new mission president, I was met by Elder James A. Cullimore and two mission assistants. After Elder Cullimore had oriented me and left the mission, the assistants said, "President, how do you feel about memorizing the discussions?" I replied, "Elders, we are going to have the greatest teaching missionaries in the Church." That night they enlisted in that particular cause. We decided we would be a Spartan mission—disciplined, obedient, frugal, spiritual, and willing to sacrifice. We wanted to be a mission that would be totally obedient and bring down the blessings from heaven to assist us in the work.

A quorum or class can have a cause—missionary work, welfare activities, activation of all quorum members, temple preparation, the bonds of brotherhood or sisterhood (unity), and dozens more. When we are involved in a united way, we achieve results we hardly dare dream.

The things we love most have the ability to become truly great causes. Families, religion, country, rights, freedoms, liberty, agency, and work—most of us prize these things dearly. In the recent war in the Persian Gulf we watched nations uniting to free Kuwait. An aggressive nation had conquered it, and the nations of the earth drove the enemy in shame back to its own homeland. On television, after Kuwait City had been freed from the ruthless enemy, there was dancing and singing, flag waving and cheering in the streets. Freedom is never so dear as when it has been taken by force. We then realize that this wonderful God-endowed blessing of liberty is more important to us than life itself.

Brave men and women from all over the world bonded together in the common cause of freedom for Kuwait. At the time this took place, I watched television news broadcasts from the distant land of the Philippines. When President Bush concluded his monumental "cease fire" speech, he said these words: "God bless all of you, and God bless the United States of America." My soul responded to that prayer.

Many of us would gladly give our lives for our countries, wherever they might be on this constantly shrinking globe.

The cause to which we throw ourselves must be real and of great worth; it cannot be fabricated. The Lord offers us many individual causes, such as baptism into the only true Church, temple sealings, eternal family relationships, missionary work, care of the needy, and our own sense of destiny, with the potential of exaltation.

When David, ancient king of Israel, was but a lad, he went to take supplies to his brothers who were warring against the Philistines. As the men of Israel explained to this young man regarding the giant of Gath, the Philistine named Goliath, and how he had defied Israel's army and Israel's God and had shamed the soldiers before each other through his challenge, David responded, "Who is this uncircumcised Philistine, that he should defy the armies of the living God?" (1 Samuel 17:26.)

David's older brother was close enough to hear David's utterance as he spoke. "And Eliab's anger was kindled against David." (Verse 28.) His anger might really have been kindled against himself when David's statement penetrated to the core of his heart. I wonder if he did not feel his own cowardice in not being willing to step forth. He vented his feelings on David, who seemed fearless. "And he said, Why camest thou down hither? and with whom hast thou left those few sheep in the wilderness? I know thy pride, and the naughtiness of thine heart; for thou art come down that thou mightest see the battle." (Verse 28.) David could have responded, "What battle? In forty days not you or anyone else here has dared to raise a sword." He might also have said, "How much longer will ye let the giant curse our God and humiliate the Lord's army? What has happened to the army of Israel, the army of Jehovah Himself? What kind of weak-kneed, cowering, sorry lot of soldiers are you?" He did not say these things. What he did say was, "What have I now done? Is there not a cause?" (Verse 29.) Indeed what a cause, but David was the only one who was willing to live or die for the cause. Only a lad, but in a short few moments he changed the attitude of the army of Israel because he reminded them of the cause. (1 Samuel 17:29.) A leader must sometimes speak with fire in his words, words that set the spirits of other men and women aflame. There must be a cause worthy of enlisting all who dare, who only need a leader and a cause.

In *Roget's International Thesaurus* under *cause* there are words such as these: *prime mover, movement, crusade, burning issue, campaign, call forth, evoke, determine, advance forward, march under the banner of,* and *fight the good fight.*

The cause is never so great as when it is based on God's eternal truths and principles. In Abraham Maslow's pyramid of what he calls the hierarchy of needs, he lists the pinnacle of motivation as self-actualization. This may be true for the outside world, but to the religious person, faith in God is the greatest motivator.

Dr. Hugh Nibley delivered an address at Brigham Young University that he entitled "Leadership versus Management." He gave the address at commencement services on 19 August 1983. It gives insight into one of the most basic needs in the Church today. The role of this Church is one of leadership. The role of the priesthood is one of leadership.

In his talk Dr. Nibley said:

> What took place in the Greco-Roman as in the modern Christian world was that fatal shift from leadership to management that marks the decline and fall of civilizations.
>
> At the present time, Captain Grace Hopper, that grand old

lady of the Navy, is calling our attention to the contrasting and conflicting natures of management and leadership. No one, she says, ever managed men into battle, and she wants more emphasis on teaching leadership. But leadership can no more be taught than creativity or how to be a genius. The Generalstab tried desperately for a hundred years to train up a generation of leaders for the German army, but it never worked, because the men who delighted their superiors (the managers) got the high commands, while the men who delighted the lower ranks (the leaders) got reprimands. Leaders are movers and shakers, original, inventive, unpredictable, imaginative, full of surprises that discomfit the enemy in war and the main office in peace. Managers, on the other hand, are safe, conservative, predictable, conforming organizational men and team players, dedicated to the establishment.

The leader, for example, has a passion for equality. We think of great generals from David and Alexander on down, sharing their beans or maza with their men, calling them by their first names, marching along with them in the heat, sleeping on the ground and being first over the wall. A famous ode by a long-suffering Greek soldier named Archilochus reminds us that the men in the ranks are not fooled for an instant by the executive type who thinks he is a leader.

For the manager, on the other hand, the idea of equality is repugnant and indeed counterproductive. Where promotion, perks, privilege, and power are the name of the game, awe and reverence for rank is everything and becomes the inspiration and motivation of all good men. Where would management be without the inflexible paper processing, dress standards, attention to proper social, political and religious affiliation, vigilant watch over habits and attitudes, etc., that gratify the stockholders and satisfy Security?

"If you love me," said the greatest of all leaders, "you will keep my commandments." "If you know what is good for you," says the manager, "you will keep my commandments—and not make waves." . . .

To Parkinson's Law, which shows how management gobbles up everything else, its originator added what he calls the "Law of Injelitance": Managers do not promote individuals whose competence might threaten their own position, and so as the power of management spreads ever wider, the quality deteriorates, if that is possible. In short, while management shuns equality, it feeds on mediocrity.

On the other hand, leadership is escape from mediocrity. The qualities of leadership are the same in all fields, the leader being simply the one who sets the highest example; and to do that and open the way to greater light and knowledge, the leader must break the mold. "A ship in port is safe," says Captain Hopper, speaking of management. "But that is not what ships were built for," she adds calling for leadership.

To paraphrase one of the greatest of leaders, the founder of this institution: "There is too much of a sameness among our people. . . . I do not like stereotyped Mormons—away with stereotyped Mormons!" (Journal of Discourses, 13:153, 8:185.) True leaders are inspiring because they are inspired, caught up in a higher purpose, devoid of personal ambition, idealistic and incorruptible." (*BYU Today,* February 1984, pp. 19, 45.)

Dr. Nibley's masterful address focuses on example. The leader must be exemplary. Years ago one young elder driving a '37 Plymouth had a flat tire on the way to the temple. He had neither a spare tire nor any time to get his tire fixed and make it to the temple. The problem occurred on 1300 East and South Temple in Salt Lake City. The young elder knew the session started in about fifteen minutes, and it was the last session for the evening. He reached into the back seat, grabbed his coat and suitcase containing his temple clothes, and started running down South Temple.

He felt conspicuous and humiliated running down the street, but he arrived just in time at the temple.

He went through the endowment session and then took a bus home after. You do not have to do much persuading in the elders quorum to get quorum members to follow a leader like that. A leader should not expect others to do that which he would not do. In fact, just the reverse is true. He expects more from himself than anyone else and generally does not look back to see who follows.

Example is in all we do. In this the leader is constant. He cannot be one level of character on the battlefield and another level when he is alone.

Dr. Nibley gives us a powerful contrast between leadership and management as he reviews Captain Moroni's attitudes and drives: "History abounds in dramatic confrontations between managers and leaders, but none is more stirring than the epic story of the collision between Moroni and Amalickiah, the one the most charismatic leader, the other the most skillful manager in the Book of Mormon. We are often reminded that Moroni 'did not delight in the shedding of blood' and would do anything to avoid it, repeatedly urging his people to make covenants of peace and to preserve them by faith and prayer. He refused to talk about 'the enemy.' For him they were always 'our brethren,' misled by the traditions of their fathers." (Ibid., p. 45.)

Isn't this a marvelous concept? He refused to talk about "the enemy": for him they were always "our brethren." The leader, even when he is criticized or hated, is still able to see the value of the person behind the attitude.

Words could not describe Captain Moroni more accurately. Again his statement, "I am Moroni; I am a leader." Dr. Nibley goes on to describe Moroni:

> He fought them only with heavy reluctance, and he never invaded their lands, even when they threatened invasion of his own, for he never felt threatened since he trusted absolutely in the Lord.

At the slightest sign of weakening by an enemy in battle, Moroni would instantly propose a discussion to put an end to the fighting. The idea of total victory was alien to him—no revenge, no punishment, no reprisals, no reparations, even for an aggressor who had ravaged his country. He would send the beaten enemy home after the battle, accepting their word for good behavior or inviting them to settle on Nephite lands, even when he knew he was taking a risk. Even his countrymen who fought against him lost their lives only while opposing him on the field of battle. There were no firing squads, and conspirators and traitors had only to agree to support his popular army to be reinstated. With Alma, Moroni insisted that conscientious objectors keep their oaths and not go to war even when he desperately needed their help. Always concerned to do the decent thing, he would never take what he called unfair advantage of an enemy. Devoid of personal ambition, the moment the war was over he "yielded up the command of his armies . . . and retired to his own house . . . in peace" (Alma 62:43), though as the national hero he could have had any office or honor. His motto was, "I seek not for power," and as to rank he thought of himself only as one of the despised and outcast of Israel. If all this sounds a bit too idealistic, may I remind you that there really have been such men in history, hard as that is to imagine today.

Above all, Moroni was the charismatic leader, personally going about to rally the people, who came running together spontaneously to his "Title of Liberty," the banner of the poor and downtrodden of Israel (Alma 46:12, 19–21). He had little patience with management and let himself get carried away and wrote tactless and angry letters to the big men sitting "upon [their] thrones in a state of thoughtless stupor" back in the capital (see Alma 60:7). And when it was necessary he bypassed the whole system, "altering the management of the affairs of the Nephites" to counter

Amalickiah's managerial skill (Alma 49:11). Yet he could apologize handsomely when he learned that he had been wrong, led by his generous impulses to an exaggerated contempt for management, and he gladly shared with Pahoran the glory of the final victory—one thing that ambitious generals jealously reserve for themselves. (Ibid., p. 45.)

I agree with Dr. Nibley regarding the qualities of a Christ-like leader compared to the motives of most managers. Dr. Nibley states, "The manager knows the price of everything and the value of nothing, because for him the value *is* the price." (Ibid., p. 46.)

Years ago, before I was called to become a General Authority, we had a top-level security expert speak to the high-level executives in our company. He made one statement that shouted volumes: "Every man or woman in this world has his or her price. It may be money, possessions, power, position, influence, riches, or something else, but everyone has his or her price." I thought of the great leaders in the Church at that time and decided the security expert was wrong. Not every man or woman has a price, but I decided he did. He had apparently seen examples of notable citizens and others who had compromised their values and principles when someone offered them "their price." Even he himself admitted that he could be bought.

Lately I have felt a great concern regarding leadership in the Church. Some local leaders in the Church seem overly interested in providing the same opportunities for all. They practice a principle illustrated by a story that I recently read. Although I do not remember the details exactly, the story went something like this:

There was an athletic competition for all the animals. There were many events sponsored. Those who organized the events felt that it was not fair that the same animals should always win particular events.

It was decided that inasmuch as the thoroughbred horse always won the sprint, he would be excluded from that event. Only turtles, beavers, armadillos, and others could enter the sprint. The thoroughbred horses and the greyhound dogs would have to enter the diving event. However, the eagles, ducks, and beavers were excluded from water events because they always won medals in swimming and diving. The kangaroos and leopards, bears and tigers were entered in weight lifting instead of the high jump. The mouse, rabbit, and raccoon were assigned the high jump, which they had never done well before. The elephant, who was great at weight lifting and always won a gold medal, was assigned to gymnastics. The giraffe was assigned to wrestling, and the cats were assigned to swim.

Every animal had the opportunity to participate in an event which they had never entered before. They were not comfortable because their attempts were contrary to their physical natures. They did not do well, and certainly no records were broken. The spectators showed no excitement because nothing spectacular happened. Medals were awarded as winners stood on the pedestal, but there was little applause and little pride felt by the animal athletes.

All the animals participated, but all were performing in events which were contrary to their God-endowed prowess.

Do you see the moral of this simple tale? We ought to let leaders lead and others serve where they perform best.

This is the Lord's work. It must move forward. The Lord endows men and women with talents, and those talents and leadership abilities ought to be put to use where they can bring about the greatest results. Knowing that God gives such gifts might be why I feel so strongly about leadership. Remember what Dr. Hugh Nibley said regarding leaders and managers: "Men who delighted their superiors (the managers) got the high commands, while the men who delighted the lower ranks (the leaders) got reprimands. Leaders are movers and shakers, original, inventive, unpredictable, imaginative, full of surprises that discomfit the enemy in war and the main office in peace."

Always the leaders will get the job done. They lift all around them. David was a leader and changed the cowardice of an entire army to courage. Captain Moroni was a leader and was willing to go to battle to protect his people.

J. C. Penney made the statement that "when the solution to any problem would come, it would always come in the form of a human being."

Great leaders will always be the solution. Leaders delight to see people who have more talent than they have. They see the outstanding traits in everyone, and they use men or women where they can accomplish the very most for the cause.

What great corporation in the world—IBM, General Motors, American Stores, Sears, McDonnell Douglas, and others—would ever take a mediocre executive and make him or her chairman of the board or president of the company? The stockholders would be incensed beyond belief! Businesses want leaders, people who are results oriented, to get the job done for them. Businesses want leaders, and they expect them to use all their talents, skills, and abilities and plumb to the depths of their energy to lead the corporation to greater productivity and profits. That requires leaders.

We ought to pray for spiritual leaders who will lift and motivate people, who will increase activity levels and performances. Why should we use a reluctant or mediocre member when we can draw from the elect and those whom God stood among and called his leaders?

Years ago I heard a story about President David O. McKay attending the dedication of a meetinghouse in Wyoming. He went into the restroom and found that members had carelessly let tissues and papers fall to the floor. Though he was dressed in his white suit, as he often was in those days, he stooped down and picked up every tissue and paper from the floor. Not a word was spoken to anyone. I do not have any idea how many lives that one story has touched, but I do know of one—mine. I think I have not been in a restroom in any meetinghouse that I have not stooped down and picked up any fallen papers from the floor. I have always wiped off the sink and counter after washing my hands. And I have told of President McKay's wonderful servant-leadership example at every meetinghouse I have dedicated.

We will find that those who have the most profound impact on our lives are those who use their leadership roles to serve. Those who are selfish, arrogant, or prideful are loathe to serve but quick to seize power. They love control, domination, and obedience by compulsion.

The Master taught the true heavenly order of priesthood leadership to His first latter-day prophet, Joseph Smith:

> No power or influence can or ought to be maintained by virtue of the priesthood, only by persuasion, by long-suffering, by gentleness and meekness, and by love unfeigned;
>
> By kindness, and pure knowledge, which shall greatly enlarge the soul without hypocrisy, and without guile—
>
> Reproving betimes with sharpness, when moved upon by the Holy Ghost; and then showing forth afterwards an increase of love toward him whom thou hast reproved, lest he esteem thee to be his enemy;
>
> That he may know that thy faithfulness is stronger than the cords of death.
>
> Let thy bowels also be full of charity towards all men, and to the household of faith, and let virtue garnish thy thoughts unceasingly. (D&C 121:41–45.)

When we analyze the principles in this wondrous counsel, we see that it is in great contrast to the world's commonly held view of leadership. To lead people by persuasion is a holy order of God. Persuasion suggests a regeneration, a change of heart, conviction, or renewal. Persuasion brings those we are leading to the same level of understanding that we have. It does not force people against their will but helps willing disciples to change; thus, the will of the persuader and the will of the persuaded become one.

Long-suffering suggests that God wants us to realize that His way in leadership is not a quick fix. We teach, train, and retrain, and then we patiently wait for the results we desired. Long-suffering is deeper than just being patient. It requires empathetic feelings and the realization that each person is different. Some may not mentally grasp a concept or principle; others may not agree and so need persuasion; still others may lack motivation. The long-suffering leader is more interested in developing and training souls than in getting the job done quicker or in some other way, or by someone else.

President Harold B. Lee often focused our attention on one word in the Lord's admonition to "let every man learn his duty." (D&C 107:99.) The word was *let*. The Christ-like life requires constant seeking and growth. Mortality provides the opportunity to gain knowledge and improve our skills. So often the best of us err but then fully realize it and are wont to change. A long-suffering leader will understand that often the process is as important as the result. This is certainly true in the life of every full-time missionary. At the close of his or her mission, the achievement of completing a full-term mission brings great satisfaction; however, the great blessing is the growth consequent to two years of varied spiritual and service experiences. It was the process that was valuable, not the goal achieved.

*Gentleness* is a word the Lord uses to describe a necessary trait for one who would use the priesthood. Usually we think of gentleness as a womanly trait. Gentleness is inoffensive, is kind, and has a softening way about it. Think of a gentle touch until you can almost feel it. In leadership, often a gentle touch creates discipleship whereas an iron hand creates rebellion. When we perform the ordinances of the priesthood—such as administering to the sick, giving blessings, ordaining or setting apart, baptizing, or preparing the sacrament—physical and spiritual gentleness is always called for.

Meekness is equally necessary. Those who are meek are absolutely submissive to God. They are teachable and have humble hearts. They are modest in their dress, speech, and service. The meek readily take on the servant-leader role. Righteousness and wisdom may come from any source, even from the lowliest among those whom they lead, and the meek acknowledge and accept it. Meekness causes us to focus on principles, that is, what is right and not who is most influential. The meek feel no need to receive credit; rather they desire to give it to those who may need it.

Love unfeigned suggests genuineness. There is no deceit, ploy, self-serving, spurious attitude in the person whose love is unfeigned. This is the type of love leaders must have. Those who exercise unfeigned love are authentic, genuine, natural, sincere, and honest. They do not flatter, nor do they distort. They are, as someone has said, "all wool and a yard wide."

To be a leader with unfeigned love has such great consequences that becoming one is in itself a supreme motivator. The Savior represented this principle in every act. Such love is a rare quality even in the Church, but it is indispensable to righteously functioning in the priesthood.

Consider again these words from Doctrine and Covenants 121:42: "kindness and pure knowledge." How can kindness and pure knowledge "greatly enlarge the soul without hypocrisy and without guile"? The term *pure knowledge* implies that all facts are uncluttered and true, with inaccuracies removed. A leader who has pure knowledge will not blunder or knowingly offend. Pure knowledge presupposes the application of justice and mercy. An effective priesthood leader must be just, and this is possible only from the vantage point of pure knowledge. Nor is mercy excluded from one who has pure knowledge. A prime example is the adulterous woman taken "in the very act," and yet mercy was extended.

Other phrases include, "Let thy bowels also be full of charity towards all men and to the household of faith." (Verse 45.) Also such words follow as *virtue, confidence,* and *doctrine of the priesthood.* These are the qualities to be desired by a leader in the kingdom of God. However, we must first desire to truly serve people before these qualities can become part of the fabric of our robe of leadership.

I am fond of a quotation that I used in another of my books. It came to me from a great Scouter, Bill (William) Gay. Bill has served on the National Executive Board of the Boy Scouts of America for years. In a talk that he gave at a national meeting, he quoted this statement by François René de Chateaubriand:

> In the days of service all things are founded.
> In the days of special privilege they deteriorate.
> And in the days of vanity, they are destroyed.

Robert Greenleaf, in his book on servant leadership, leads us through this great concept. Of course, it is not new; the prophets have always understood, valued, and followed it. Indeed, the Savior taught His Twelve Apostles: "Ye know that they which are accounted to rule over the Gentiles exercise lordship over them; and their great ones exercise authority upon them. But so shall it not be among you: but whosoever will be great among you, shall be your minister: And whosoever of you will be the chiefest, shall be servant of all." (Mark 10:42–44.)

Servant leadership is based on a profound respect for the children of men. It requires leadership traits that do not demean, debase, or otherwise cause those we lead to feel inferior. Servant leadership lifts, blesses, and changes lives in a positive way.

Years ago I was touring a mission in the South. The ward Relief Society sisters had provided a lunch. They had set up more than a hundred chairs along with the tables. Decorations adorned each table, which were covered with paper. At the end of the lunch, the missionaries were all standing in the cultural hall visiting. The custodian, who was a woman, came in and began to clean up. She started folding chairs and putting them away. I watched for a moment to see if any elder would assist her. No one did. I went to her and told her we would put the chairs away. She seemed relieved. I began to fold chairs and put them away. Within moments the mission president and twenty to thirty missionaries had joined me. We had the chairs and tables stored and the room cleaned within minutes.

There may be some who would say, "What is a General

Authority doing putting away chairs?" I would respond, "I was helping a dear sister with a needed task." The question might also be asked, "Then why didn't you just assign the elders to do it?" Again I would respond, "No one had to be told; each one out of his own volition chose to assist." Isn't that servant leadership? Even if not one other elder would have assisted, my own personal standards would not have let me stand by while this sister performed such a heavy labor alone.

Servant-leaders exercise the following traits and practices in their roles. They:

- Understand the value of every human soul.
- Have an inborn or developed sense of caring for others.
- Are quick to volunteer to take pressure off someone else.
- Rush to the aid of someone who is going through an embarrassing or humiliating experience.
- Treat all people on a basis of equality.
- Do not feel that tasks they expect others to do are too demeaning for themselves.
- Are not offended by disruptions of people who are themselves going through emotional traumas or stress.
- Expect more from themselves than they do from anyone else.
- Are quick to compliment, give credit, and build up those who perform a given task.
- Judge people by their potential, not necessarily by one single negative experience.
- Do not take credit for someone else's achievements and love to share credit for any of their own accomplishments.
- Get the facts before finding fault or criticizing another person.
- Help all people feel they had a real part in the success of a project.
- Detest practical jokes or statements that focus humiliation or attention on one soul.
- Always constructively criticize in private and compliment in public.

- Are absolutely honest in their work.
- Are equally fair with all under their direction.
- Are always willing to listen to both sides of a quarrel, discussion, or issue. They know it is a pretty thin pancake that has only one side.
- Set an example in controlling costs and are conservative.
- Make themselves accessible to all, not just those with position or power.

True servant-leaders do not need a checklist of these character traits, for they live them daily. I feel strongly about the necessity of servant-leaders treating all with equality. I have heard some secretaries who have been instructed that when the phone rings, they are to first find out who is calling. If the caller has the right name or position, then he or she is permitted to speak with the secretary's boss. However, if the caller lacks influence or is unknown, he or she is not permitted that privilege. Some aspiring leaders are available only to those over them or those who can influence their future. To avoid this appearance, I have always made it a practice to have my secretary not ask a caller's name until after she has informed the caller whether I am in and available. If I am in a meeting, she takes a message and says, "He will call you back as soon as he can." If I am available, she says, "Yes, I will put you through. May I tell him who is calling?"

I know of cases where a young missionary needing a visit with a priesthood leader has come to his office for an appointment. The missionary sat waiting outside the office three hours after his appointment was scheduled. Whenever anyone makes an appointment with a servant-leader, that time belongs to that person. I treat a transgressing missionary with the same respect as I do a stake president. I would not keep a stake president waiting, and I will not keep the missionary waiting either. The fact that a person has been less faithful in keeping his or her covenants than another does not give me license to treat him or her with less consideration. Of course, the counseling will be different, but a person is a person, created in the image of Almighty God. (Lest I be misunderstood, I realize that emergencies can come up that legitimately must alter scheduled appointments on occasion, but even then consideration should be extended to those involved as explanations are given and rescheduling taken care of.)

President Howard W. Hunter was a tremendous servant-leader. I recall Elder Neal A. Maxwell's telling of being in Israel with President Hunter. He awakened at an early hour to find President Hunter shining Elder Maxwell's shoes for him. President Hunter's total life was one of servant leadership. It was contrary to his nature to be authoritative, dictatorial, unfair, critical, or prejudiced.

So many people imposed or seemed to impose on the Master's time and energies. Consider the palsied man who could not get into the house because it was full. They took the palsied one up on the housetop, "and let him down through the tiling with his couch into the midst before Jesus." (Luke 5:19.)

Who may know what Jesus was teaching at that precise moment? Undoubtedly it would have been some pearl of great price. Those who lowered the man with palsy before Jesus apparently had not considered anyone but their friend. They did not hesitate to interrupt the Master Teacher, disrupt all who had gathered to hear the message, and remove part of the roof tile to lower the man through. A modern-day equivalent might be someone bursting into a meeting of the First Presidency, the Council of the Twelve, and other General Authorities to seek help for a personal need. Yet the Savior showed no anger, no offense. He knew the hearts of these people, so he healed the man and told him to take up his couch and go to his home.

Servant-leaders are leaders because they are servants first of all. Servant-leaders might not be properly recognized by those of greater influence and might even be ridiculed as was Jesus for healing the palsied man. Nevertheless, the people always know who the real leaders are.

Servant-leaders also understand the uniqueness and individualism of each person. Years ago I remember hearing the Greek legend of Procrustes. The legend referred to a "Bed of Procrustes." It was six feet long. Those who were not six feet tall were stretched to fit the bed. Those who were over six feet had the excess inches lopped off. Everyone was expected to fit the Procrustean Bed. That is fortunately not the way of the Lord or His kingdom. He has always called uncommon men and women with great integrity, ambition, discipline, and faith in Christ. Not all will fit in the same size bed, nor will all fit into the same callings.

Everyone will not—and should not—be the pinnacle leader at the ward, stake, or general Church level, but everyone can make his or her maximum contributions as a servant-leader in a particular calling and circumstance. And that is all the Savior expects of us—our very best, wherever we are.

## CHAPTER THIRTEEN

# To Touch the Hem of His Garment

Oh, what a blessing God gave to us through His Only Begotten! No one who ever brushes against the teachings and ministry of Jesus will ever be the same. They may choose not to accept His gifts beyond measure, but they will never forget Him.

I would like to share some thoughts about an issue of blood and an issue of tears. One of the most touching of all Jesus' miracles came as a result of hearing of miracles. A woman had had an issue of blood for twelve years. I think of this story often because of the tenderness of the situation. (Luke 8:43–48.) Imagine any human soul having a constant fountain of bleeding. Consider the physical limitations this would place on the one so afflicted, the draining of her energy and health day after day, year after year. The woman must have been weak, pale, and anemic. She had been to various physicians over the years, none of whom had brought relief. She had spent all of her money and undoubtedly was nearly destitute.

She may well have come near losing all hope. When hope dies, we die. Hope is essential to life's continuance. In our mind's eye we may catch a glimpse of her in her home. We see her desperate, heartsick, weak, and ill. Even she must have questioned why she had to go on living.

Somehow in this final state of hopelessness, she heard about one Jesus of Nazareth who was healing the sick, causing the blind to see, the deaf to hear, the leprous to be cleansed. A fountain of hope must have sprung up inside her heart. She learned of His being nearby. Surely, she put on the best of her poverty-governed wardrobe and hurried to where He was supposed to be. At last, she saw Him amid the throngs of people. The disciples were near Him, and everyone was jostling, pushing, trying to get closer. Some were curious; others loved Him and followed out of reverence; still others hoped for a blessing.

This woman, seeing the Master, thought, "If I but touch the hem of His garment, I will be healed." How it was that she mustered the strength to push through the crowd to get close enough to touch Him, we may never know. Drawing close, she reached out and was able to do no more than touch His garment. Immediately the blood was stanched. We picture the woman, sinking back into the crowd and perhaps even dropping to her knees in gratitude. The Savior halted and said, "Who touched me?" Everywhere people were pressing and pushing, brushing against him constantly, and so the disciples responded that many people had touched Him, for they were pressing on all sides. However, only one had really touched Him. He turned and saw the woman, who must have known He was questioning after her. I suppose the suddenness of the blood being stanched, the Master's stopping, the crowd quieting down to hear what He was saying, and the full attention being drawn to this woman would have been more than she could bear. She must have felt as if she were spotlighted on center stage. Rapt attention of all the crowd focused on her. She may even have felt guilty.

Luke's record of the event states, "Jesus said, Somebody hath touched me: for I perceive that virtue is gone out of me." (Luke 8:46.) Again we consider Jesus' sensitivity to know and feel a "healing" virtue leave Him. He knew that someone had, through faith, drawn healing from the well of His soul and had more than brushed against Him.

"And when the woman saw that she was not hid, she came trembling, and falling down before him, she declared unto him before all the people for what cause she had touched him, and how she was healed immediately." (Verse 47.)

He undoubtedly detected her guilt, embarrassment, or humiliation and said, "Daughter, be of good comfort: thy faith hath made thee whole; go in peace." (Verse 48.)

What a comfort, what solace, what power in the few simple words of the Master of heaven and earth! The peace she received may have been equal to the healing blessing. When the Son of God blesses with peace, it is an absolute fact that peace will come. Nor could the crowd find fault, for He said, "Go in peace."

Though not recorded in scripture, undoubtedly the halting of the issue of blood was followed by an outpouring of an issue of tears. It usually takes an issue of tears to prepare us for the benefits of the Atonement. It would be a blessing to all of us if somehow we could close out the final pages of our book of life without ever having smudged or otherwise marred the pages. Too often, though, we find those who have been involved in serious transgression. Furthermore, all of us sin to a greater or lesser degree, and we will all be tried.

President Harold B. Lee shared a great truth during his conference talk in April 1950. He said: "It is my conviction that every man who will be called to a high place in this Church will have to pass these tests not devised by human hands, by which our Father numbers them as a united group of leaders willing to follow the prophets of the Living God and be loyal and true as witnesses and exemplars of the truths they teach." (Conference Report, April 1950, p. 101.)

The Apostle Paul gave us a lifeline as he declared in 1 Corinthians 10:13: "There hath no temptation taken you but such as is common to man: but God is faithful, who will not suffer you to be tempted above that ye are able; but will with the temptation also make a way to escape, that ye may be able to bear it."

What did President Lee mean when he said that we "will have to pass through tests not devised by human hands"? What does it mean to "make a way to escape"? This life provides an opportunity for us to use our agency. It appears from President Lee's statement that there will be a special testing for those who will walk in high places. The testing may well be unique to us. And, of course, the greatest trials we face have to do with the things we love the most—our families, our church, our religion, our leaders, our country, and our friends. These things have the potential of hurting us most.

"Not devised by human hands" suggests that the Lord has His own program for purifying and preparing His leaders. Many of us feel that we have been refined in the Lord's crucible more often than we would want, had we a choice. It is not easy to be between the hammer and the anvil. But we must remember always what Paul said: "[God] will with the temptation make a way to escape, that ye may be able to bear it." It is my opinion that this same principle applies to tests and trials we face. They will never be greater than we can withstand.

We find how resilient our souls are. We find out how far we can bend and still not break. The Lord knows us better than we know ourselves, and He is constantly molding us to the grand design of His great expectation and divine destiny. We will always come through testings as a more valued human soul. Each trial brings out the "steel and velvet" in us, as someone has said. Our commitment to the absolute truths of the gospel puts a steel in us that can endure tremendous pressure. On the other hand, the suffering brings about a velvet softness, a Christ-like charity. Suffering or testing, trials or troubles, sinsickness or soulsickness—all take us through our own personal issue of tears.

Years ago I was at an inn in Tennessee. The inn had a special hall where world-renowned Tennesseeans were honored. The walls were covered with plaques and portraits of the men and women who had left an impression on the past and were honored and beloved in the present. One of those men was Walter Malone, who had written a poem entitled "Opportunity." May I share it with you?

### OPPORTUNITY

They do me wrong who say I come no more
When once I knock and fail to find you in,
For every day I stand outside your door
And bid you wake, and rise to fight and win.

Wail not for precious chances passed away,
Weep not for golden ages on the wane!
Each night I burn the records of the day;
At sunrise every soul is born again.

Laugh like a boy at splendors that have sped,
To vanished joys be blind and deaf and dumb;
My judgments seal the dead past with its dead,
But never bind a moment yet to come.

Though deep in mire, wring not your hands and weep;
I lend my arm to all who say "I can!"
No shamefaced outcast ever sank so deep
But yet might rise and be again a man.

Dost thou behold thy lost youth all aghast?
Dost reel from righteous retribution's blow?
Then turn from blotted archives of the past
And find the future's pages white as snow.

Art thou a mourner? Rouse thee from thy spell;
Art thou a sinner? Sins may be forgiven;
Each morning gives thee wings to flee from hell,
Each night a star to guide thy feet to heaven.

    (IN RALPH L. WOODS, ED., *A TREASURY OF INSPIRATION*
    [NEW YORK: THOMAS Y. CROWELL CO., 1951], P. 83.)

I have quoted portions of this poem to members of the Church the world over. I believe with all my heart in its principles. The star of hope is essential in the eyes of all humanity. It may dim and flicker, but it must remain if we are to survive. Walter Malone's marvelous poem provides hope and teaches eternal truths. It is a special gift for all who feel inadequate, unloved, unwanted, or unimportant. John Wesley quoted his mother, I believe, who said to him:

> Do all the good you can,
> By all the means you can,
> In all the ways you can,
> In all the places you can,
> At all the times you can,
> To all the people you can,
> As long as ever you can.

This is another gift we all can give. There is no qualifier in this marvelous statement regarding those whom we serve—just everyone, all the time, with all we have. Certain truths ring to the center of our beings. The statement by John Wesley is one of them.

In Mark 10:29–30 the Lord talks to the unwearying Saints who serve: "There is no man that hath left house, or brethren, or sisters, or father, or mother, or wife, or children, or lands, for my sake, and the gospel's, but he shall receive an hundredfold now in this time, houses, and brethren, and sisters, and mothers, and children, and lands, with persecutions; and in the world to come eternal life."

C. S. Lewis gave a gift to all who are endlessly doing good and blessing their children, and who later find the children blaming their faults and weaknesses on Mom and Dad. Those children put us on a guilt trip and lay a shadow on our heart that is with us twenty-four hours a day. In his book *The Great Divorce*, Lewis taught a principle that is a blessing to myriads of souls: pity and guilt cannot forever hold us hostage. There are those who wallow in their pity. The only misplaced joy they get is in the guilt they can place on others. This happens in unhappy marriages, those who transgress and rebel, those who commit suicide. They get even by laying guilt on all those they leave behind. The only satisfaction they get is knowing that husbands and wives, fathers or mothers, teachers or bishops will forever have a void that guilt or pity places on them. (P. 12.)

C. S. Lewis suggested that the demand of the loveless and self-imprisoned cannot be allowed or permitted to blackmail the universe or hold others at hostage until they consent to be happy. This, they suppose, has to be on their terms, not anyone else's, that somehow hell should be able to veto heaven's blessings.

Could it be that after we have done all we can to reconcile and make peace with those we may have offended that there does come a time when their tyranny will have no power over us? This may sound cruel when we think of a son or daughter—a Laman or Lemuel, Absalom or Cain—but even those we love most dearly, our family members, must not have power to forever darken our joy. One day we will have God's love, which is eternal love. There can be no shadow that would or could darken our joy for eternity, for that would not be just. What a marvelous gift that concept is. We can begin to practice it in righteousness in this life. The Master said, "Ye shall know the truth, and the truth shall make you free." (John 8:32.)

Another marvelous gift is that of life itself. The Savior of heaven and earth was born in what was described as a lowly stable. He was "wrapped in swaddling clothes and laid in a manger." (Luke 2:7.) As humble as that beginning was for Jesus, we have births as humble today. Jesus was loved by Mary and Joseph. Mary knew that he was physically, literally, the Son of God. Joseph had had a heavenly manifestation that let him know of the divine destiny of this babe born of his espoused wife. We suppose Joseph would lay clean hay or straw down as well as make everything as comfortable as possible.

I once read in the newspaper of two births. One of the babies, a girl, was put into a plastic bag and stuffed into a garbage can. The other was discarded similarly in a trash bin. Both babies were found only hours after birth and survived.

Just after the turn of the century, Brother Cobbley in Pleasant Grove, Utah, was working in his yard. It was the fall of the year. He was raking leaves. The previous year Brother and Sister Cobbley's teenaged son was killed. Sister Cobbley grieved greatly and could not get his death off her heart. Brother Cobbley, while raking the yard, noticed a burlap sack that someone had thrown over the fence into his garden. He took his pitchfork and was about to run it through the sack to throw it onto the pile of leaves, when suddenly he heard a muffled sound. He opened the sack, and there was a beautiful baby girl just a few hours old. He took her into the house. The mother, who had been grieving, had her heart healed by the spirit of mercy that overwhelmed her. She said, "This is our gift from God."

They had ten or twelve children. They put the name of each child into a hat. The child whose name was drawn out would have the privilege of naming the baby. The fifteen-year-old son's name was drawn. He must have obtained a book of names and name meanings. When he made his decision, he said, "We will call her Dorothy because Dorothy means 'gift of God.' "

This little soul grew up in the Cobbley home. She was loved without measure. They said she was like Pollyanna—she was always happy. She was a vivacious, healthy child in grade school and was popular in high school. Many said she was one of the most beautiful girls in the school. She was always kind and warm to everyone.

She also had the good sense to date young men with promise and a love for the Lord. She married one of these in the Salt Lake Temple. When they came out of the temple, they walked down to the A&W root beer stand on Fifth South and State Street (I believe), and had a five-cent root beer and a hamburger. That was their wedding breakfast. Then the couple went to eastern Idaho, where the new husband went into the grocery business.

Years later this young man and his father had several stores in the Northwest. They sold them, and he went to work for Safeway. One day the founder of Safeway, L. S. Skaggs, called this man into his office. He made Dorothy's husband an offer that reflected on the value of the man. He gave him a check for one million dollars and told him they were going into business together. He said they would share the profits fifty-fifty. L. S. Skaggs was to furnish the money, and Dorothy's husband was to manage the business. It was a great success. Dorothy's husband became wealthy. He never forgot the Church. He served as a stake president, a regional representative, a temple president, and a General Authority of the Church. Dorothy Cobbley had married O. Leslie Stone, who served as an Assistant to the Twelve and as a member of the First Quorum of the Seventy. What a great and precious gift is the gift of life, however humble the beginning.

Another special gift I would wish for each of us is the gift of sight and the use of it. We see much in this life. How we use this precious gift of sight is part of our gift to God.

### If You Know a Tall Man

If you know a tall man out ahead of the crowd,
A leader of men marching fearless and proud,
And you know a tale which the mere telling aloud
Would cause his proud head in shame to be bowed,
It's a pretty good plan to forget it.

If you know of a skeleton hidden away in a closet,
Guarded and kept from the day in the dark,
Whose showing, whose sudden display,
Would cause grief and sorrow and lifelong dismay,
It's a pretty good plan to forget it.

If you know of a spot in the life of a friend,
We all have such spots concealed world without end,
Which the shame of its telling no grieving could mend,
It's a pretty good thing to forget it.

If you know of a thing that would darken the joy,
Of a man or a woman, a girl or a boy,

That would sadden or in the least way
Annoy a fellow or cause gladness to stray,
It's a pretty good plan to forget it.

(ANONYMOUS.)

We see much of what people do. Some things are not worthy of them. We might occasionally see conduct not becoming a Latter-day Saint. Do we also see all of the wonderful things that people do around us? There is so much good in people. If we are watching for that goodness, we will see it. If we watch for faults, we will see them. How much better to look for the good. We ought to use our sight to the greatest advantage.

Reading is a marvelous gift. When we read, we can be in an instant at the temple in the land of Bountiful or at the foot of King Benjamin's tower. We can stand shoulder to shoulder with Captain Moroni with our own "title of liberty." We can be in a sacred grove with Joseph Smith or at Christ's birth with Mary and Joseph.

We can see in our mind's eye all the great goodness of God's creations, traveling by book from one land to another. We can stand with Winston Churchill during World War II or walk onto the shore with General Douglas MacArthur and General Carlos Romulo when he returned to the Philippines. What a blessing it is to read!

Elder Marion D. Hanks stated that on a tombstone in a cemetery in Switzerland is an epitaph that reads: "Here lies a man who was straight and true and wise as a chest of old books."

The lyrics in the "Blind Plowman" speak of "God, who took away my sight that my soul might see." But God should not have to take away our sight for us to receive spiritual insight. Rather, let us use both types of sight to bless others.

Another gift, when used properly, is our ability to communicate. Oh, what power and sweetness, what love and strength is in the human voice! We have the potential to speak and bless so many lives. J. S. Lewis shared with us a song that has been a gift to all who have heard it:

## Oh, I Had Such a Pretty Dream, Mama

Oh I had such a pretty dream, Mama,
Such pleasant and beautiful things;
Of a dear little nest,
In the meadows of rest,
Where the birdie his lullaby sings.

A dear little stream full of lilies,
Crept over the green merry stones,
And just where I lay,
Its thin sparkling spray
Sang sweetly in delicate tones.

And as it flowed on toward the ocean,
Thro' shadows and pretty sunbeams,
Each note grew more deep,
And I soon fell asleep
And was off to the island of dreams.

I saw there a beautiful angel,
With crown all bespangled with dew;
She touched me and spoke,
And I quickly awoke,
And found there, dear Mama, 'twas you."
(J. S. Lewis, *Deseret Sunday School Songs*, p. 184.)

We can make such beautiful memories with words, even though there are some things that cannot be described: "No tongue can speak, neither can there be written by any man, neither can the hearts of men conceive so great and marvelous things as we both saw and heard Jesus speak." (3 Nephi 17:17.)

"Memories" as someone has said, "come surging back into the heart to make it clean or to accuse it."

We may speak a word of comfort to someone struggling that may be more important than we would ever suppose. Each Christmas I consider and ponder deeply over the gifts of God.

Usually I speak somewhere to some group, as much for me as for them. It is in the preparation of Christmas talks that I feel deeply of the Spirit.

Our family has Christmas traditions, as do you. Some are recognized and are labeled as Christmas traditions. Some are repeated year after year but somehow are not gathered onto a list of our traditions.

Like many people, we decorate our house inside and out. We have three wise men, wonderfully created and standing about eighteen- to twenty-four inches tall. They have been part of our decorations for about thirty years. We keep them in a large trunk at home. One year when our daughter was staying in our house, she found them and put them on the piano for Christmas. That is where we generally put them. Their faces are sculptured and detailed, filled with character. She knew that was what her mom would want.

We decorate the railings and have manger scenes, wreaths, other miniature Christmas scenes, and all else that an imaginative and creative woman can dream up during the year.

On Christmas Eve we read from the second chapter of Luke and *The Other Wise Man,* by Henry Van Dyke.

Some of us who no longer have to put toys together will watch a videotape or a television program of Handel's *Messiah.* We will watch *It's a Wonderful Life,* starring Jimmy Stewart, and shed a few tears. We will see *Mr. Krueger's Christmas* and hopefully *The Miracle on 34th Street.* Cookies and 7–Up will be prepared for Santa Claus (he doesn't like milk at our house). There are also some traditional (not on the list) things that I do. I always love to listen to "O Holy Night," "The Holy City," and "Ave Maria" (in our Church the lyrics are "Heavenly Father"). I love the smell of cinnamon rolls baking early in the day and a turkey baking on Christmas Eve. I like to be at home on Christmas Eve, so we go visiting, delivering gifts, and singing carols a few days before.

I also like to have some calorie-loaded eggnog and Mrs.

Cavanaugh's chocolates, and I love when it snows. I like to sit up late with a fire in the fireplace, just content not to have to do a great deal. That is also a gift we earn.

No Place to Go

The happiest nights
    I ever know
Are those when I've
    No place to go,
And the missus says
    When the day is through:
"To-night we haven't
    A thing to do."

Oh, the joy of it,
    And the peace untold
Of sitting 'round
    In my slippers old,
With my [favorite] book
    In my easy chair,
Knowing I needn't
    Go anywhere.

Needn't hurry
    My evening meal
Nor force the smiles
    That I do not feel,
But can grab a book
    From a near-by shelf,
And drop all sham
    And be myself.

Oh, the joy of it,
    Oh, the comfort rare,
Nothing on this earth
    To it can compare.

## OUR MODEL

And I'm sorry for him
Who doesn't know
The joy of having
No place to go.
(Edgar A. Guest, *A Heap o' Livin'*
[Chicago: Reilly and Lee Co., 1916], pp. 110–11.)

I am convinced that the gift of peace to enjoy a time when you can relax is also a gift of God. There is a sweet time of rest for the laborer.

Let me conclude with a final gift we all have—the gift of friends. Oh, what a blessing it is to have a good friend! In section 121 of the Doctrine and Covenants, the Lord responds to Joseph Smith's humble pleading and praying that the Lord, with his "sword [would] avenge us of our wrongs" and that "thy suffering saints . . . will rejoice in thy name forever." (D&C 121:5–6.) The Savior comforted Joseph and referred to Job's trials. Job had lost his camels, his sheep, his asses, and much more. He had lost all of his children when the wind blew down his house. He also suffered carbuncles and boils. However, the thing that the Lord focused on when comforting Joseph was that "thy *friends* do not contend against thee . . . as they did Job." (D&C 121:10; emphasis added.)

Friends are essential, and blessed is the man or woman who has close friends. We had a dear friend who was also our bishop. His name was Paul Pehrson. He was a "man after [God's] own heart," as David was described. (1 Samuel 13:14.)

We had a young man in our ward named Dan Baker. Dan was a teenager. He lived with a younger sister and his mother. I believe his parents were divorced. They went through some difficult times. Dan played the piano, and he played it well. He was not just talented but exceptionally so. The mother had to sell the piano when conditions grew tough financially. Dan did not complain, although it nearly broke his heart. But it broke his mother's heart a thousand times more. She knew what the piano meant to the life of a boy without a father and with a poor self-image. However, she had no choice. In order to survive, they had to sell the piano.

A few days before Christmas a nice used piano was delivered to the home of the Bakers. It was a Christmas present from an anonymous giver. We found out by accident that the giver was our bishop, Paul Pehrson.

That same year we decided we would order Christmas through a catalog. We all selected what we wanted. We sent the order in two or three months before Christmas. The week before Christmas, the order had not yet arrived. About 99 percent of our family's Christmas was on that order. I comforted my wife and told her that the company was a prominent one—they would know that was our Christmas order, and it would be delivered on or before 24 December. It was not. We waited until late in the afternoon, and still there was no delivery. To me it was incomprehensible that such a business would not perform. Merlene and I were aching inside. Somehow I think I felt like my mom did all those Christmases when she couldn't give us everything we ordered or even anything we wanted.

I do not remember whether we had to get Paul Pehrson to open up his hardware store just for us or not. I only remember that we met him there, and we bought gifts for each of our sons, all five of them. I had no way to get the money to him that night; I did not have enough in my account, and no bank was open where I could get a loan. He never even raised the subject—but I did. I asked him if I could pay him after I had obtained a loan. He was kind beyond belief. We had a Christmas that year because of a bishop who was one of the dearest friends we have ever had.

You need only one friend like Paul Pehrson to be endowed with a great gift. I suppose, looking back, that there were hundreds and hundreds of people who felt that Paul Pehrson was a close friend.

The purchases from the catalog never did come. In February we received a letter asking if we still wanted our order filled.

We sometimes sing of the twelve days of Christmas; here are the thirteen gifts that we have considered in this chapter:

- The gifts of an issue of blood and an issue of tears
- The gift of testing
- The gift of having "a way to escape"
- The gift of the opportunity to start over and be clean
- The gift of hope
- The gift of self
- The gift of being free from guilt that others try to place on us
- The gift of life itself
- The gift of sight to see the things of God and to read
- The gift to communicate and to bless through our words
- The gift of having traditions, both listed and unspoken
- The gift of rest for those who deserve it
- The gift of friends

These are thirteen gifts of Christmas we might consider this year, but the greatest of all God's gifts is eternal life. And that gift is available to all who ever have, do now, or will yet walk the earth. Only a few will receive it. He who trod the winepress alone invites all to enter His Father's kingdom.

What a wondrous announcement a single star hanging over Bethlehem made! What a beautiful concept is a Christ-centered Christmas! Let us give the gifts of Christmas all year round. We may be tested with an issue of blood or an issue of tears, but we will be tested. And when we are, let us always remember that through faith we can reach out, "touch the hem of his garment," and be healed.

## CHAPTER FOURTEEN

# Having Christ's Image in Our Countenance

In the third year of the reign of Jehoiakim king of Judah came Nebuchadnezzar king of Babylon unto Jerusalem, and besieged it." King Nebuchadnezzar "spake unto Ashpenaz the master of his eunuchs, that he should bring certain of the children of Israel, and of the king's seed, and of the princes." (Daniel 1:1, 3.)

Then King Nebuchadnezzar set a standard for the young men to be considered. He wanted "children in whom was no blemish, but well favoured." (Verse 4.) This would suggest he wanted strong, robust young men who were healthy, energetic, and had high energy levels; young men who were well proportioned, with a comely or handsome appearance.

He was also desirous that they be skillful in all wisdom. (Verse 4.) That is quite a requirement for a young man. Elder John H. Vandenberg has said, "Wisdom is the fruit which ripens slowly." (Conference Report, April 1969, pp. 17–18.) However, nearly every community has some young men who seem to have good judgment and more than average wisdom for their age. "Skillful in wisdom" suggests that they would know when and where to use their wisdom. In addition, he wanted them to be "cunning in knowledge." (Verse 4.) To be cunning in knowledge might imply that someone be a plotter or sly in the use of information. Knowledge benefits us most when it can be used properly. Many people have accumulated great amounts of knowledge, but they do not always use it in a positive way. Sometimes their knowledge remains a seldom-used bank of information. Apparently the king wanted knowledgeable young men who also had the wit to use that knowledge for his purposes.

It was necessary, according to the king's standard, that those selected have an understanding of science. (Verse 4.) In the broad sense, the king must have thought of the sciences of earth and nature, heavens and stars, chemistry, language, mathematics, and constant laws of the universe.

King Nebuchadnezzar wanted those who could "stand in the king's palace." (Verse 4.) Those selected would be expected to be confident, assured, dignified, portraying a proper image, and at ease with nobility. Also the king planned on having them learn the "tongue of the Chaldeans." (Verse 4.) A quick and bright intellect with the discipline to study hard would be necessary.

In one paragraph, King Nebuchadnezzar set a high standard for those who would be chosen: "Children in whom was no blemish, but well favoured, and skilful in all wisdom, and cunning in knowledge, and understanding science, and such as had ability in them to stand in the king's palace, and whom they might teach the learning and the tongue of the Chaldeans." (Daniel 1:4.)

The king had a special interest in this group. He appointed them a daily provision of the king's meat and of the wine that he drank: for three years he planned to nourish them in this way so that at the end they might stand before him. (See verse 5.)

Among those selected were the children of Judah, Daniel, Hananiah, Mishael, and Azariah. Now, the name of Daniel we know, but who were Hananiah, Mishael, and Azariah? Actually the prince of the eunuchs gave new names to all four. He changed

Daniel's name to Belteshazzar. This seems to have made little difference, for down through the ages, Daniel is the name that follows his prophetic role. The names given to Hananiah, Mishael, and Azariah were Shadrach, Meshach, and Abed-nego. Of course, these are the names by which we remember these three Hebrew lads.

Daniel is described as having an "excellent spirit," and indeed he did. He made up his mind that he would not defile himself with the king's meat or the king's wine. This was the finest meat and wine procurable. It was the very food and drink of the king himself. Regularly dining on this bounteous feast was a privilege extended to few in the kingdom.

Daniel went to the prince of the eunuch and requested that he might not be brought to defile himself. (Daniel 1:8.) God had brought Daniel into favor of the prince of the eunuchs. The prince desired to grant Daniel's request, but his fear of the king was greater than his love for Daniel. The eunuch said, "I fear my lord the king, who hath appointed your meat and your drink: for why should he see your faces worse liking than the children which are of your sort? then shall ye make me endanger my head to the king." (Verse 10.)

Then Daniel said to Melzar, whom the prince of the eunuchs had set over Daniel, Hananiah, Mishael, and Azariah, "Prove thy servants . . . ten days; and let them give us pulse to eat, and water to drink. Then let our countenances be looked upon before thee, and the countenance of the children that eat of the portion of the king's meat: and as thou seest, deal with thy servants." (Verses 12–13.)

Pulse, according to the Bible Dictionary, refers to seeds, including grains of leguminous vegetables or any other edible seeds.

Melzar took away the portion of their meat and the wine that they should drink, and gave them pulse. "As for these four children, God gave them knowledge and skill in all learning and wisdom: and Daniel had understanding in all visions and dreams." (Verse 17.)

At the end of the allotted time, "the prince of the eunuchs brought them in before Nebuchadnezzar. And the king communed with them; and among them all was found none like Daniel, Hananiah, Mishael, and Azariah: therefore stood they before the king. And in all matters of wisdom and understanding, that the king enquired of them, he found them ten times better than all the magicians and astrologers that were in all his realm." (Verses 19–20.)

Consider that these four young men were *ten times better*. They were part of an elite, hand-selected group who were the best of the best. Imagine being ten times better than all the others who were also hand selected.

Nebuchadnezzar then dreamed a dream that troubled his spirit. He was unable to sleep, and he could not recall the dream. He commanded the magicians, the astrologers, and the sorcerers to make known his dream. They responded, "O king, live for ever: tell thy servants the dream, and we will shew the interpretation." (Daniel 2:4.)

But the dream was gone from him. That was part of the problem. King Nebuchadnezzar threatened their lives if they were unable to recall his dream and interpret it. The king could see behind the deceit and cunning of the astrologers and sorcerers. Only he in all the world would know the dream. The astrologers, magicians, and sorcerers had no possible way to find out what the king's dream was. There was no way that chicanery, tricks, or deceit could take place. He would recall the dream when someone through a special power could relate it to him.

When Daniel heard that the decree had gone forth to have the wise men slain, he went to Arioch, captain of the king's guard, who was assigned to slay these wise men. "Then Daniel went in, and desired of the king that he would give him time, and that he would shew the king the interpretation." (Verse 16.) Then Daniel went to his house and made known to Shadrach, Meshach, and Abed-nego what he had done. They were anxious that the tender mercies of God would reveal the secret that they might not be slain. "Then was the secret revealed unto Daniel in a night vision. Then Daniel blessed the God of heaven." (Verse 19.)

There was only one power on earth or in heaven that could reveal the dream, the God of heaven. Daniel praised His name. Then Daniel taught the overruling power of God and said: "Blessed be the name of God for ever and ever: for wisdom and might are his: and he changeth the times and the seasons: he removeth kings, and setteth up kings: he giveth wisdom unto the wise, and knowledge to them that know understanding: He revealeth the deep and secret things: he knoweth what is in the darkness, and the light dwelleth with him." (Daniel 2:20–22.)

Then Daniel sought Arioch and asked to be brought before the king. The king said to Daniel, "Art thou able to make known unto me the dream which I have seen, and the interpretation thereof?" (Verse 26.)

Daniel wanted the king to remember that the magicians, the astrologers, the sorcerers, and the soothsayers could not know the secret. Then Daniel declared:

> But there is a God in heaven that revealeth secrets, and maketh known to the king Nebuchadnezzar what shall be in the latter days. . . .
>
> As for thee, O king, thy thoughts came into thy mind upon thy bed, what should come to pass hereafter: and he that revealeth secrets maketh known to thee what shall come to pass.
>
> But as for me, this secret is not revealed to me for any wisdom that I have more than any living, but for their sakes that shall make known the interpretation to the king, . . .
>
> Thou, O king, sawest, and behold a great image. This great image, whose brightness was excellent, stood before thee; and the form thereof was terrible.
>
> This image's head was of fine gold, his breast and his arms of silver, his belly and his thighs of brass,
>
> His legs of iron, his feet part of iron and part of clay.

Thou sawest till that a stone was cut out without hands, which smote the image upon his feet that were of iron and clay, and brake them to pieces.

Then was the iron, the clay, the brass, the silver, and the gold, broken to pieces together, and became like the chaff of the summer threshingfloors; and the wind carried them away, that no place was found for them: and the stone that smote the image became a great mountain, and filled the whole earth.

This is the dream; and we will tell the interpretation thereof before the king.

Thou, O king, art a king of kings: for the God of heaven hath given thee a kingdom, power, and strength, and glory. . . . Thou art this head of gold. (Daniel 2:28–38.)

He then describes inferior kingdoms until the last days. Then he envisions our day:

And in the days of these kings shall the God of heaven set up a kingdom, which shall never be destroyed: and the kingdom shall not be left to other people, but it shall break in pieces and consume all these kingdoms, and it shall stand for ever.

. . . the great God hath made known to the king what shall come to pass hereafter: and the dream is certain, and the interpretation thereof sure. (Daniel 2:44–45.)

This is a great prophecy for the latter days. King Nebuchadnezzar fell upon his face, worshipped Daniel, and commanded that great privileges come to him. He also declared to Daniel, "Your God is a God of gods, and a Lord of kings, and a revealer of secrets." (Verse 47.)

Then the scripture states that King Nebuchadnezzar made Daniel a great man. In reality, no one can make someone else great. Daniel was already great, and the king merely honored him.

Every time Daniel was honored, he also lifted Shadrach, Meshach, and Abed-nego.

It is a marvelous privilege to associate with good and holy people, those who have determined their course in life and have the integrity to follow it at all costs. Daniel was living proof to these three young men that God is only a whisper away to his true servants.

In Daniel 3, these three young men would face their own test—life threatening and horrible.

King Nebuchadnezzar made an image of gold. It is likely that he received the idea from his dream. The image was three score cubits high (approximately ninety feet) and six cubits wide (about nine feet). He set it up in the plain of Dura. King Nebuchadnezzar invited all the princes, governors, captains, judges, treasurers, counsellors, sheriffs, and rulers to come to the dedication of the golden image.

When all had gathered, a herald cried aloud, "To you it is commanded, O people, nations, and languages, that at what time ye hear the sound of the cornet, flute, harp, sackbut, psaltery, dulcimer, and all kinds of musick, ye fall down and worship the golden image." This was followed by a threat that "whoso falleth not down and worshippeth shall the same hour be cast into the midst of a burning fiery furnace." (Daniel 3:5–6.)

Everyone complied with the king's decree except Shadrach, Meshach, and Abed-nego. Certain Chaldeans made this known to the king. They rehearsed the king's decree and punishment and made their accusations against the three Hebrew princes.

King Nebuchadnezzar, in his rage and fury, commanded Shadrach, Meshach, and Abed-nego to be brought before him. The command and threats were reaffirmed. He said, "If ye worship not [the golden image], ye shall be cast the same hour into the midst of a burning fiery furnace." And then Nebuchadnezzar taunted them, "And who is that God that shall deliver you out of my hands?" (Verse 15.) How quickly he had forgotten, and Daniel was not there to remind the king. Indeed who is that God?

Shadrach, Meshach, and Abed-nego answered, "We are not careful to answer thee in this matter. If it be so, our God whom we serve [not just worship] is able to deliver us from the burning fiery furnace, and he will deliver us out of thine hand, O king. But if not, be it known unto thee, O king, that we will not serve thy gods, nor worship the golden image which thou hast set up." (Verses 16–18.)

King Nebuchadnezzar was furious; he commanded that the furnace be heated seven times more than it was usually heated. He commanded the most mighty men that were in his army to bind these three Hebrew princes and cast them into the burning fiery furnace. Then these men were bound in their coats, their hose, their hats, and their other garments, and the three godly men were cast into the midst of the furnace.

The flame was so hot that the men who cast Shadrach, Meshach, and Abed-nego were slain by the heat, and these three men fell down in the midst of the burning fiery furnace.

To the king's great astonishment, he saw not only the three young men but also a fourth who was like the "Son of God." (Verse 25.)

Nebuchadnezzar came near to the furnace and spake, "Shadrach, Meshach, and Abed-nego, ye servants of the most high God, come forth, and come hither." (Verse 26.) Then Shadrach, Meshach, and Abed-nego came forth out of the midst of the fire. They had not been harmed; not even a single hair of their head had been singed. Their coats were not changed, and there was no smell of fire.

Then Nebuchadnezzar said, "Blessed be the God of Shadrach, Meshach, and Abed-nego, who hath sent his angel, and delivered his servants that trusted in him, and have changed the king's word, and yielded their bodies, that they might not serve nor worship any god, except their own God." (Verse 28.) Then the king made a decree that no one should speak against the God of Shadrach, Meshach, and Abed-nego.

So much is left unsaid. What about the Chaldean informers?

Can you imagine they would creep back into their holes where the jealous, aspiring, prideful, and evil lurk?

Where was Daniel during this great event? There is little question that his presence would have made a difference. However, the Lord in his great love and condescension let Shadrach, Meshach, and Abed-nego go through their own trial of faith. No one has done it better. They were magnificent in defying the king's command even at the peril of their lives.

Remember that when they were selected, they were "children in whom was no blemish, but well favoured, and skilful in all wisdom, and cunning in knowledge . . . and such as had the ability in them to stand in the king's palace." (Daniel 1:4.)

In the end, they were more than that—they stood in royal priesthood dignity before the king and defied him with power and assurance. Not even his kingly authority could force them to compromise the least or greatest commandments of God.

The names Hananiah, Mishael, and Azariah will be emblazoned in the eternities for all to honor, for these three great men and Daniel had Christ's image in their countenance and His law in their hearts.

## CHAPTER FIFTEEN

# Becoming Prisoners of His Love

The Lord's Church is unique in a thousand ways or more. Every member has an opportunity to lead and serve. Many leaders remain unheralded, yet their contribution is of great significance to the kingdom. Men and women who lead together do a work considerably greater than either of them could do alone. So it is with missionary couples. They complement each other in their roles. No worthy Latter-day Saint should refuse to answer this clarion call to lead, however limited his or her leadership skills. Let us focus on a special segment of the Church.

I would write to our generation—those from World War II and the wars in Korea and Vietnam who have served country, God, and man—a sweetly naive generation, a generation that did great things but had the wisdom not to talk about them much. There is another need for us now.

This cause is of such great consequence that the Savior, in His final instructions to His disciples, charged them with it: "Greater love hath no man than this, that a man lay down his life for his friends. . . . I have chosen you . . . that ye should go . . . and that your fruit should remain." (John 15:13, 16.)

Never has the Church had a greater need than now for an army of mature couples to go to every corner of this earth and retain the fruit of the harvest. The harvest is truly great and the laborers are few. Remember the words of Ammon: "Our brethren, the Lamanites, were in darkness, yea, even in the darkest abyss, but behold, how many of them are brought to behold the marvelous light of God! And this is the blessing which hath been bestowed upon us, that we have been made instruments in the hands of God to bring about this great work." (Alma 26:3.)

Imagine what thousands of couples could do this year, followed by hosts more in succeeding years. We could move into the fields of harvest and nurture, care for, and gather them "into the garners, that they are not wasted. Yea, they shall not be beaten down by the storm at the last day." (Alma 26:5–6.)

I think we will not be tested in the way that the pioneers were tested. They were called to leave all worldly possessions, homes, even family and loved ones to cross the prairies to dry, desolate, and forbidding lands. They buried their babies, children, and companions on the Great Plains in shallow, unmarked graves. Physically, they suffered beyond belief, nor can tongue tell their sad and pitiful story. Out of the ashes of their sacrifice, this kingdom has emerged to become the most powerful force for good on the face of the earth today.

There is a need not to leave homes and properties forever, but for a time, and then to return and reap the rich harvest of the faithful laborer. Your children and grandchildren will be blessed. The power for good will go out from Zion, and the world will truly acknowledge "how beautiful upon the mountains are the feet of him that bringeth good tidings; that publisheth peace." (Mosiah 12:21.)

Can you imagine any more Christ-like service than to secure the harvest? Missionary couples are sent into the branches to minister and nurture. They strengthen the Church; they "lift up the hands that hang down" (D&C 81:5); and they fall in love with Filipinos, Africans, Norwegians, Haitians, Polynesians, east, west, south, and every far reach of the earth. Imagine what it means to be truly needed by the Lord in a far ministry.

There was a popular song that our generation will remember. Entitled "A Prisoner of Love," it spoke of a love so great that the writer felt he simply had to serve his beloved. So it may be for more mature missionaries. Wonderful couples who simply love the Lord and will enlist in this great work and accept a call will also be prisoners of love—His love.

René de Chardin said: "Someday, after we have mastered the winds, the waves, the tides, and gravity, we will harness for God the energies of love: and then, for the second time in the history of the world man will have discovered fire."

Alcibiades said of Socrates: "He is the only man who can make me feel ashamed. I know I ought to do what he tells me, but when I am out of his presence I don't care what I do and yet I have been bitten by something more poisonous than a snake—I have been bitten in the heart and the mind." I have been bitten in the heart and mind with love.

Wilferd A. Peterson suggested: "A master at the art of living makes no distinction between his work and his play, his labor and his leisure, his mind and his body, his education and his recreation, his love and his religion. He hardly knows which is which. He simply pursues with excellence what he is about and leaves others to determine whether he is working or playing. He himself knows he is always doing both."

And Yogi Berra, a baseball player renowned as a great American philosopher, said, "When you come to a crossroads . . . take it."

You may have reached a crossroads. Now is the time to accept a call or volunteer for one.

An elderly woman at a rest home turned to the old man next to her and said, "I can guess your age." He said, "You can't." She replied, "Yes, I can. You go take a bath, shave, brush your hair, put on a nice clean shirt and tie, and shine your shoes. Then I'll tell you." The little old man was gone for an hour. When he returned, he was neat, clean, hair brushed, shoes polished, and in his suit. She said, "Now you go stand up against the wall." He said, "All right, now how old am I?" She replied, "You're eighty-nine." He responded, "That's right, but how did you know?" She said, "You told me yesterday."

After examining an older man, a doctor said to the man's wife, "I don't like the looks of your husband." "Neither do I," the woman said, "but he is good to our children."

Some of us may look a little old, but if we get all dressed up, we don't look half bad.

Can you imagine what a wonderful blessing it would be to serve in a branch in Alaska, Barbados, Haiti, Nigeria, Manila, Stockholm, or Tennessee? We need couples filled with love and a desire to serve, whose chief responsibility is to bless the harvest so that the fruit will remain. Experience alone from a mature life of service qualifies us to become nurturers.

Thanksgiving, Christmas, and New Year's will never be the same again once you have celebrated them while serving a mission. Imagine a small Christmas tree with a few decorations, Christmas carols, a humble apartment—it all adds up to create a Christmas spirit that makes that little apartment seem a sacred temple. Brethren, you will never be more in love with your wife than when you pack your white baptismal clothing and walk hand in hand to the chapel where a little family waits patiently to enter God's kingdom through the waters of baptism. You see the star of wonder not hanging over Bethlehem but in the eyes of humble, sweet converts. You look at your wife, she looks at you; nothing need or can be said; both of you are overcome with joy.

The twelve or eighteen months you serve will seem as a small moment, but the memories will last through the eternities. Those of us who have partaken of the goodness of God have a divine charge to share what we have received.

The Apostle Paul declared to the Ephesians: "Know the love of

Christ, which passeth knowledge, that ye might be filled with all the fulness of God." (Ephesians 3:19.)

We should be filled with all the fulness of God. We ask along with James: "What doth it profit, my brethren, though a man say he hath faith, and have not works? can faith save him?" (James 2:14.)

And in the last verse of the book of James, the apostle gives us a key to our service: "Let him know, that he which converteth the sinner from the error of his way shall save a soul from death, and shall hide a multitude of sins."

Should the reward be less for the nurturer, the garner, the caretaker? President Harold B. Lee taught that only as we make ourselves totally available are we worthy disciples of Christ. And yet another promise reaches beyond us. We worry and ache and hurt over family members who have erred. Doctrine and Covenants 31:5 provides a great challenge and promise: "Therefore, thrust in your sickle with all your soul, and your sins are forgiven you, and you shall be laden with sheaves upon your back, for the laborer is worthy of his hire. *Wherefore, your family shall live.*" (Emphasis added.)

Ours has been a giving generation. Why not one more time, that our families should live? We do not know the blessings or condescensions of God. However, the promise is sure, "Wherefore, your family shall live." Blessings will come to our wayward or wandering children, even those who are married and have children of their own.

Our generation came through horrible times—World War II, Korea, and Vietnam. We now live in the season of the world when good has become evil and evil good. We have heard outcries against the things we hold precious and dear—prayer and God. We see attempts at legalization of drugs, abortion, homosexuality, and other compromising, drifting philosophies. Some of the brightest in our generation have been swept by giant waves onto treacherous shoals. We may not have been all that we should have been as parents, but we have loved our children, our Church, and our country, and we have cared for people in all nations. Some of the best blood of our generation has been spilled to preserve freedom. We have sacrificed many things to provide those who would follow with better than we had. This may well be another opportunity to reach our own by serving others.

There is a holy hand behind the divine purposes of God. We can be His "instrumentalities." Most of us do not have many years left to live. As we come to the later years of life, we come to a mature spiritual understanding. We have these next years to do something great, important, and significant for God, our religion, and our families. We ought to raise a new title, not of liberty, but of love—a banner that will remain long after we are gone.

What better way have we to prepare to meet our God than to serve a mission when the autumn and winter of life are upon us?

We are prisoners of love. Come, my beloved brethren and sisters. Let our generation do something great and noble; come join our ranks. Let us march by the thousands out into the vineyard to nurture, teach, and bless the tender branches. Let us protect and bless the fruit of the harvest. Let us gather the sheaves into the garners, away from the storm, safe from the whirlwind, a holy place where the storm cannot penetrate.

A good man said, "I believe the test of a great man is humility. I do not mean by humility the doubt in one's own personal power; but really, truly great men have the curious feeling that greatness is not in them but through them and they see the divine in every other human soul and are foolishly, endlessly, incredibly merciful."

That sounds like our generation. Who knows but what God will grant for us and ours what we do for others. Come, lift your banner high, and march with us into the mission field in the spirit of love and caring.

Begin to prepare. Ponder and pray together. Our generation can do something great for those who follow. Have we been "steeled" for the very purpose about which I have been speaking? Let the ranks of missionaries swell with couples from every broad reach of this earth that the fruit will remain.

## CHAPTER SIXTEEN

# Christ, Our Constant Inspiration

O ver the years the Spirit has touched my life. The influence of
the Spirit lifts us to more noble deeds and thoughts. That
influence can be felt in many ways, and often we struggle to
express the deep, sweet, wonderful emotions attendant to the
Spirit. In this short chapter, I have assembled a few poems on various themes that attempt to make such expression.

Some years ago I spoke at Brigham Young University about
the sufferings of the Martin Handcart Company and other pioneer
trials. It inspired me to write this poem:

THEY ALL CAME THROUGH IN GLORY

In July's hot sun,
The trek begun,
    The handcart companies toiled.
With oxen to goad,
And heavy load,
    Their faces strong and soiled,
They built and tooled,

They pushed and pulled,
    Till wearily they fell.
They toiled and sweat,
Till dripping wet,
    They bid the past farewell.
Up and down,
No golden crown,
    The dust rose up in clouds.
From early dawn,
They toiled on,
    The cold around them shrouds.
The very best
Continued west,
    With all they owned they came.
Proud men,
Greater then,
    Stripped of pride and shame.
But the trials grew,
The windstorms blew,
    Came soon the dreadful foe.
Ice and cold,
Testing young and old,
    In whiteness fell the snow.
After labored breath,
With night came death;
    Brave souls lay in the grave.
Free of greed,
They shared indeed,
    But more, their lives they gave.
Frostbite came
And made some lame;
    Others never walked again.
Laid to sleep,
In snow knee deep,
    The roughest, toughest of men.

## OUR MODEL

At night's end,
Death was their friend,
    Nor breathed they evermore.
Relief had come,
Life was done,
    Swept to an eternal shore.

Those still spared,
Less well they fared,
    For the crucible was fired white.
They wept and froze,
In their tattered clothes.
    Angels blessed them through the night.
Food grew scarce,
Life more sparse,
    A moment seemed like a life.
Yet they lost not faith
While fearing death
    Of daughter, son, or wife.
With rags wrapped 'round
Their feet were bound;
    The penetrating cold still chilled.
The wolves came too
And dug graves through,
    Their starving stomachs filled.
Then from far away
Came help that day,
    With men, wagons, and supplies.
And great tears shed,
Over a loaf of bread,
    While brave rescuers wiped their eyes.

Now saw they light
Through darkest night,
    For the caring brethren came.
Westward they streamed,

As they had dreamed,
    Came forth the cold and lame.
Through mountains steep
Where snow drifts deep,
    Their goal was almost reached.
Soon their valley home,
Under heaven's dome,
    Lay before them on deserts bleached.
To the valley floor,
Through the open door,
    To loving homes they came.
The pudding and bread,
To souls almost dead,
    Was as manna to their frame.
And now the years
Have dried the tears
    Of the pioneer stories we tell.
Let us not forget
The trials they met
    Were the bitterest tests of hell.
For their faith proved true
For me and you,
    And they all came through in glory.
The heart doth melt
For the tests they felt
    In the brave pioneer handcart story.

Over time I have watched the spirit of patriotism wane. Other than at athletic events, we seldom sing patriotic songs, nor do we recite the Pledge of Allegiance. We must teach our children patriotism, a marvelous character trait of great people. The following poem expresses my deep feelings for my homeland. I wrote it taking inspiration from statements by Abraham Lincoln and Captain Moroni, lest we forget.

# OUR MODEL

For Freedom Burned in Heart and Bone
(A Call to Patriotism)

Of latter nations on the earth
 The one to me of greatest worth
Is my own dear, beloved land
 Whose place with ancient empires stand.
White stars adorn her noble flag;
 It will not fade, nor will it sag.
For heroes brave have shed their blood
 And fought in snow and cold and mud.

Young men to battle stations went,
 While wives and mothers not content
To sit and watch their loved ones die,
 With tear-stained cheek and moistened eye,
Became a source of strength ne'er matched
 By any army ere dispatched.
For freedom burned in heart and bone,
 And brave, great men dared stand alone.
And so the patriotic ten
 Became a hundred million men
Who swore before the throne of God
 That no foreign foot would ever trod
By force upon one inch of land
 Kept sacred by a loyal band
Of Christians who were strong and true
 And did what God would have them do.

So hail our land, long may it be
 The ensign of our liberty.
May every man down to the last
 Match men of courage from the past.
God bless our nation, keep her free,
 Guard well her human dignity.

And grant that we may never falter
    For brave men's hearts lie on her altar.

The next poem is inspired by my own dear mother. President Benson and his wife, President Hinckley and his wife, and President Monson and his wife all attended the viewing for this beautiful woman I love and honor and call Mother. Many of the Twelve and Seventy attended the funeral of this Saint, insignificant to the world and yet terribly important and loved by eight children. To honor her I wrote these words:

### MOTHERS

Her children were her crown and glory;
    A simplistic life, a common story.
Her silver locks imbued with beauty
    Golden once, now white from duty.
She served in all she did each day
    The tide of "men" who crossed her way;
Her constant caring touched each life
    In joy or peace or endless strife.
She tended children and loved each one,
    Prepared the meals till day was done.
She washed and ironed and ever shared;
    She swept and vacuumed and always cared.
Some good she sought to do each day;
    Her food she shared in every way.
She had little sleep and far less rest,
    Her life an endless trial and test.

The years extracted from this wife
    Energy and strength, her very life.
And so the motherly gift she'd given
    Was a golden path that leads to heaven.
Her children, friends, and all she met
    Were swept into her loving net.

## OUR MODEL

And when her life's last breath was spent,
    Her eyes were closed in sweet content.
Honored by both the great and small,
    They came to weep, her friends and all.
Another mother's life was o'er,
    Not rich, not great, but wise and sure.
Blessed by God so sweet and fine,
    A mother pure, God's grand design.

The next verse was inspired by my love for good and righteous leaders. The greatest examples of leadership in my life have come from within this magnificent and wonderful Church.

### THE LAW OF THE LEADER

The law of the leader is irrefutably true;
    He will accomplish what others dare not do.
Where do we find the qualities to lead?
    The law of the leader says examine the deed.
For a leader will always comply with the law
    Of committing himself with a resolute jaw.
He is fearless and tireless; he's faithful and true;
    He works longer and harder than lesser men do.
He breaks not a commitment and always comes through,
    A "go getter," do better, inspired and true.
His law is to succeed whatever his cost,
    For life to him in the wide world would be lost
If he dared not lead out and aid other men
    To take giant strides and be heroes again.

These next two poems were inspired by Christ's ministry and how it influences our lives. Hopefully, one or more of these might be an inspiration to someone, somewhere, sometime.

### THE HOPE OF THE WORLD

The light in my life is a constant one,
    A holiness that shrouds me till daylight is done.

It's the warmth in my soul, the light in my eye;
    It's a fire . . . a shining . . . till the day that I die.

Oh Master, dear Master, how may I show
    My love, my commitment, my feelings, and oh . . .
How then can one who has felt of Thy power
    Be without it a moment, an instant, an hour?

Thou comfortest my soul; Thy balm's healing love
    Is distilled on Thy servant like rains from above.
Oh Jesus, my Savior, my soul would be lost
    If Thy light, which surrounds me, o'er my path ne'er
    crossed.

Thou art my beacon, my light from the shore,
    The glow in my countenance, my hope evermore.
Who am I that can abide in Thy love,
    Which rests on my soul like a soft cooing dove?

Take me, mold me as clay in Thine hand;
    Refine me and purge me, help me to stand . . .
As a bastion, a pillar, a disciple, and now
    A pilgrim, a servant, a healer like Thou.

And so as I pray and serve through this life,
    The depths of my soul, my toil and my strife,
Oh help all the helpless, oh bless all the poor;
    Bless all who would serve Thee with life evermore.

### I MET AN OLD MAN
### (A POEM FOR CHRISTMAS)

I met an old man who was worn out and gray;
    His eyes were sunken and hollow.
And yet there was something in his old withered face
    That bid to me, come and follow.

I followed by day and I watched by night
    Till I knew his constant direction.

# OUR MODEL

His pathway was set, for always he sought
    To live charity to its utmost perfection.
Like the other wise men, he had gifts to share;
    His king he sought through his deeds.
Conrad the Cobbler was an inspiration to him;
    He searched for each soul's urgent needs.

Sir Launful's adventure to search for the grail
    Kept his footsteps turned toward his Lord.
His goodness expanded with each passing day,
    Ministering by act, deed, and word.

The poor wayfaring man of grief was his theme;
    He shared bread crust, water, and bed.
He attended the lonely, the widow, and orphan
    Wherever his ministering led.

In Eden's Garden he lay down to sleep;
    Another dawn he never would see.
Then out of the heavens he heard the sweet voice,
    "Come, sweet Pilgrim, come unto me."

As the Spirit touches us, we soften, modify, change. Our lives become more substantial, and we reach out to all who have loved us or who have needed us or whom we have needed. Our goal is to be "even as He is" and to become brothers and sisters in Christ. How we express that goal and our feelings about it are manifest in many ways. My hope is that these few verses will move you to feel the Spirit more deeply and, in turn, to find some way to express that feeling to lift others around you.

## CHAPTER SEVENTEEN

# Mormon, A Man of Christ

Perhaps no prophet's name is used for good or evil more than *Mormon*. The humble, converted Latter-day Saint can hardly receive a greater compliment than to be called a Mormon. To the ignorant, the biased, the wicked, *Mormon* is a despicable term, a despised people, a feared religion.

Mormon himself was quite a man. He was unique in the annals of history. When he was ten years old, Ammaron, who was the keeper of the sacred records of the Church, visited him. In our day, a boy of ten is in the fourth or fifth grade. He has not yet reached adolescence. Quite often he has never been away from home and may still be afraid of the dark. Ten is a very tender age to be approached by a holy man of God and be given a sacred trust that would carry through his lifetime. Filling that trust would bring him adoration, undying love, and respect; it would also prepare him for his role as prophet-leader.

Ammaron had watched the lad and seemed to know him well. "I perceive that thou art a sober child, and art quick to observe," he said. (Mormon 1:2.) It is my feeling that some traits come trailing down from the premortal life with us. Reverence for God is something that brings the soberness that Ammaron knew was part of Mormon's life, tender as his age was. Ammaron had also described him as being "quick to observe." In my mind I see a boy who is obedient and who tried diligently to do all that his parents, teachers, and other authority figures would have him do. It was unlikely they would have had to labor with him over and over; rather, his young, bright mind must have quickly grasped what he was taught, and he simply believed.

Ammaron charged him, saying, "When ye are about twenty and four years old I would that ye should remember the things that ye have observed concerning this people." (Mormon 1:3.) This says much about the confidence Ammaron had in Mormon. Mormon was supposed to observe, remember, and record what transpired during the next fourteen years. What are the things that would impress a person who is ten, thirteen, seventeen, twenty, twenty-four? How much of the ministry of the kingdom would an adolescent or teenager be involved in or even notice? He would be guided by the things he heard his elders, teachers, and parents discuss, which would then be filtered through his own experiences and observations. Mormon was true to the trust.

Ammaron continued, "When ye are of that age [about twenty-four] go to the land Antum, unto a hill which shall be called Shim; and there I have deposited unto the Lord all the sacred engravings concerning this people . . . and ye shall engrave . . . all the things that ye have observed concerning this people." (Verses 3–4.) At that young age, would our minds have comprehended the implications of this brief charge? Yet Mormon remembered and heeded perfectly Ammaron's words.

To Mormon, this charge or assignment from Ammaron was a commandment. He recorded later what he had observed during those fourteen years. When he was eleven, the family moved to Zarahemla. Young Mormon described what he saw there: the whole face of the land had become covered with buildings, and the population as numerous as the sands of the sea. Apparently during his eleventh year war broke out. His quickness to observe is evident. He stated that the allied forces of the Nephites, Jacobites, Josephites, and the Zoramites warred against the Lamanites, Lemuelites, and Ishmaelites. This was over nine hundred years after Lehi had left Jerusalem with his family. The posterity of Nephi, Jacob, Joseph, and Zoram had apparently kept their ties to each other. The descendants of Laman, Lemuel, and Ishmael also banded together. Interesting that a young boy would be aware of the divisions of the warring factions. He then reduced the opposing armies to broader political designations of Nephites and Lamanites. The Nephite army of 30,000 slew many Lamanites in that battle.

For four years, Mormon recorded, there was peace. It was an uneasy peace, however, as this young lad showed his spiritual awareness by declaring that "wickedness" prevailed. Miracles and healings ceased because of the iniquity of the people. That is extremely insightful for a young teenager. Mormon said, "There were no gifts from the Lord, and the Holy Ghost did not come upon any, because of their wickedness and unbelief." (Verse 14.) Not unlike Joseph the Prophet, when Mormon was fifteen, "he was visited of the Lord, and tasted and knew of the goodness of Jesus." (Verse 15.)

Mormon attempted to preach, but he was forbidden because the people had willfully rebelled against God. The three Nephite disciples were taken away out of the land because of the people's iniquity. It thrills me that Mormon called them "beloved" disciples. He undoubtedly knew them, and they knew him. He must have had a special reverence for them. They probably personally told him they were leaving. They must have known the charge that had been given to young Mormon by Ammaron. It brings joy to my soul to know that Mormon brushed against these three holy men of God other times during his ministry.

The Gadianton band of robbers was revived by the master of secret combinations to work its evil purposes. Mormon in his youth described treasures that had become "slippery"; sorcery, witchcraft, and magic became popular; and "the power of the evil one was wrought upon all the face of the land." (Verse 19.) These evils, Mormon declared, fulfilled the words of Abinadi and Samuel the Lamanite. Mormon must have been a good student and comprehended the scriptures well. He knew the words of the prophets. Although we cannot discern directly from the Book of Mormon record, it is not out of line to suppose that much of this understanding and mature judgment resulted from his relationship with the beloved disciples and other teachers.

Mormon was large in stature as well as spirit. When he was but fifteen (in his sixteenth year), he was "head of an army of the Nephites." (Mormon 2:2.) The Lamanites came upon Mormon and his army with exceedingly great power. Though Mormon was not afraid, his army was. Possibly had Mormon been more experienced he could have rallied his army to stand and battle rather than retreat. Later on we see that his experience gave him victories over larger opposing armies.

Young Mormon described the blood and carnage that had spread throughout the robber-infested land both on the part of the Nephites and the Lamanites.

The Nephites found they could not keep what they owned because of the thieves, robbers, murderers, and the magic art and witchcraft. There was great mourning and lamentation. Mormon rejoiced as the people of Nephi seemed to begin repenting and mourning. His only desire was that the Nephites become a righteous people. However, his joy was shortlived, "for their sorrowing was not unto repentance . . . ; but it was rather the sorrowing of the damned, because the Lord would not always suffer them to take happiness in sin." (Mormon 2:13.)

Mormon was approximately thirty-three when this took place. He had the spiritual maturity to judge the people's motivation. He wrote of "broken hearts and contrite spirits" as absent signs of devotion and repentance; rather, the Nephites cursed God and wished to die. (Verse 14.)

Mormon described sorrowfully how they struggled with the

sword for their lives: "I saw that the day of grace was passed with them, both temporally and spiritually; for I saw thousands of them hewn down in open rebellion against their God, and heaped up as dung upon the face of the land." (Verse 15.)

To a prophet, spiritual death and suffering are far more grievous to the soul than temporal suffering and death. Mormon was faithful, sensitive, and committed to the Lord. Imagine how painful it must have been to have under his command generals, captains, and leaders who cursed and defiled all that Mormon held dear.

Keeping his promise to Ammaron, Mormon continued the record-keeping with which he had been charged, explaining that "a continual scene of wickedness and abominations has been before mine eyes ever since I have been sufficient to behold the ways of man." (Verse 18.) How old would he have been when he was "sufficient" to behold the ways of man? Possibly eight, nine, or ten?

Mormon could no longer appeal to his people to fight in the name of their God, but he did appeal to them to "stand boldly before the Lamanites and fight for their wives, and their children, and their houses, and their homes." It took this to "arouse them somewhat to vigor." The Nephites then took their army of 30,000 against an army of 50,000 with such firmness that the enemy fled before them. (Mormon 2:23–26.)

Mormon describes the greater calamity "of my people because of their wickedness and their abominations." (Verse 27.) These are the things that cause great souls to grieve.

A treaty then enters the story, bringing peace for ten years. During that period the Lord said to Mormon, "Cry unto this people—Repent ye, and come unto me, and be ye baptized, and build up again my church, and ye shall be spared." (Mormon 3:2.) Mormon did what the Lord commanded him, but it was all in vain.

Bringing an end to this decade-long peace, the king of the Lamanites sent an epistle to Mormon. The Lamanites were preparing to do battle against the Nephites. However, when they came, Mormon's military preparations and cunning brought victory to his army, and the Lamanites were turned back. A year later they came again, and again they were turned back. But rather than thank their God for their success, the Nephites boasted of their own strength and swore before heaven, and also by the throne of God, that they would go up and cut the Lamanites off from the face of the earth.

Mormon could stand such mockery no longer and refused to be the military commander for the Nephites. They had dishonored what he held precious and dear. Mormon described how he felt about his people: "I had led them many times to battle, and had loved them, according to the love of God which was in me, with all my heart; and my soul had been poured out in prayer unto my God all the day long for them. . . . And thrice have I delivered them out of the hands of their enemies, and they have repented not." (Mormon 3:12–13.) This gives us some indication of his depth of commitment and feeling towards his people, but it was to no avail.

"And when they had sworn by all that had been forbidden them by our Lord and Savior Jesus Christ, that they would go up unto their enemies to battle, and avenge themselves of the blood of their brethren, behold the voice of the Lord came unto me saying: Vengeance is mine, and I will repay; and because this people repented not after I had delivered them, behold, they shall be cut off from the face of the earth." (Verses 14–15.) Mormon could no longer lead such an army. He stood as a witness of the things which he saw and heard. Mormon would have been about fifty-one at this time. You can imagine what a mighty man he was. He had been the commander of all the Nephite armies since he was fifteen. He was large and had fought powerfully for his people. He had had many victories and always gave credit to the Lord.

A year later, the Nephites went forth to battle against the Lamanites but were driven back to the land of Desolation. (Mormon 4:1.) While they were weary, a fresh army of Lamanites came upon them, and a "sore battle" commenced. Many prisoners were taken by the Lamanites, and the remainder fled. Mormon must have watched this horrible scene in a state of hopelessness. He knew that the Nephites had lost the support of God. Then Mormon gives marvelous insight from years of experience: "It is by the wicked that the wicked are punished." (Mormon 4:5.) This applies to our day—abortion, homosexuality, AIDS, dishonesty, violence. "It is by the wicked that the wicked are punished." In our day, the wicked transmit diseases to one another, perform nonjustifiable abortions, and kill or maim each other in barroom brawls.

When Mormon was fifty-five, he wrote, "It is impossible for the tongue to describe, or for man to write a perfect description of the horrible scene of the blood and carnage which was among the people, both of the Nephites and of the Lamanites." (Verse 11.) Every heart had been hardened, and Nephite and Lamanite alike delighted in the shedding of blood. "There never had been so great wickedness among all the children of Lehi, nor even among all the house of Israel." This was not Mormon's appraisal but was "according to the words of the Lord." (Verse 12.)

Mormon then watched while Nephite women and children were offered up as sacrifices to idol gods by the Lamanites. (Verse 14.)

So great was the anger of the Nephites that they went to battle against the Lamanites and did beat them and drive them out of the land. Mormon would have viewed this great scene with pain, sorrow, and disgust. The people he had loved and led for more than forty years were now totally godless. There were brief victories on either side, and then the Lamanites "slaughtered them with an exceedingly great slaughter and their women and children were again sacrificed unto idols." (Verse 21.)

As the Nephites fled from before the Lamanites, Mormon went "to the hill Shim, and did take up all the records which Ammaron had hid." (Verse 23.)

Finally Mormon repented of his decision to no longer help his people, and they gave him command of their armies. They looked to him as if he could deliver them from their afflictions. "But behold, I was without hope," said this great prophet-leader. (Mormon 5:2.) They repented not, nor did they turn to God. Mormon was sixty-eight or sixty-nine years old, but still a mighty warrior, commander of all the armies. Under Mormon's leadership, his army fought valiantly, but it was all in vain: the Lamanites were so numerous that they did "tread the people of the Nephites under their feet." (Verse 6.) Mormon beheld scenes of horror and violence so great that he would not write about them, so that "ye might not have too great sorrow because of the wickedness of the people." (Verse 9.)

Mormon lamented his people, who had become dark, loathsome, and filthy, yet "they were once a delightsome people, and they had Christ for their shepherd; yea, they were led even by God the Father." (Mormon 5:17.) Then the prophet looked down the channels of time and called the Gentiles, who would one day scatter the Lamanites, "to repent and turn from their evil ways." (Verse 22.)

When Mormon was seventy-four, he finished his record. He wrote to the king of the Lamanites and asked that he allow the Nephites to gather together in the land of Cumorah to give battle. The Lamanite king granted the request. Mormon hid the records that he had kept "in the hill Cumorah." (Mormon 6:6.) He gave a few plates to Moroni, his son; then the armies of the Lamanites came marching forth. Every soul was filled with "that awful fear of death which fills the breasts of all the wicked" because of the greatness of the Lamanite numbers. (Verse 7.) They came with sword, bow, arrow, ax, and all manner of weapons of war. Mormon, with his 10,000 men, was hewn down. He lay wounded in the midst, and they did not put an end to his life. They had hewn down all but twenty-four, among whom was Moroni; 10,000 each led by Moroni, Gidgiddonah, Lamah, Gilgal, Limhah, Jeneum, Cumenihah, Moronihah, Antionum, Shiblom, Shem, Josh, and ten more with their 10,000 did fall by the sword. More than 230,000 were slain of the Nephites. (Verses 11–15.)

Beholding nearly a quarter of a million of his people slain, Mormon cried out:

> O ye fair ones, how could ye have departed from the ways of the Lord! O ye fair ones, how could ye have rejected that Jesus, who stood with open arms to receive you!
>
> Behold, if ye had not done this, ye would not have fallen. But behold, ye are fallen, and I mourn your loss.
>
> O ye fair sons and daughters, ye fathers and mothers, ye husbands and wives, ye fair ones, how is it that ye could have fallen!
>
> But behold, ye are gone, and my sorrows cannot bring your return.
>
> And the day soon cometh that your mortal must put on immortality, and these bodies which are now moldering in corruption must soon become incorruptible bodies; and then ye must stand before the judgment-seat of Christ, to be judged according to your works; and if it so be that ye are righteous, then are ye blessed with your fathers who have gone before you.
>
> O that ye had repented before this great destruction had come upon you. But behold, ye are gone, and the Father, yea, the Eternal Father of heaven, knoweth your state; and he doeth with you according to his justice and mercy. (Mormon 6:17–22.)

What a heartrending plea from a great general, prophet, father, and husband! Then again looking down through the channels of time, Mormon spoke to the latter-day Lamanites and appealed to them to believe that Christ is the Son of God, concluding: "Ye will also know that ye are a remnant of the seed of Jacob; therefore ye are numbered among the people of the first covenant; and if it so be that ye believe in Christ, and are baptized, first with water, then with fire and with the Holy Ghost, following the example of our Savior, according to that which he hath commanded us, it shall be well with you in the day of judgment. Amen." (Mormon 7:10.)

The records are left to Moroni, who stated that his father was slain in battle and then filled his own charge regarding the records:

> Therefore I will write and hide up the records in the earth; and whither I go it mattereth not.
>
> Behold, my father hath made this record, and he hath written the intent thereof. And behold, I would write it also if I had room upon the plates, but I have not; and ore I have none, for I am alone. My father hath been slain in battle, and all my kinsfolk, and I have not friends nor whither to go; and how long the Lord will suffer that I may live I know not. (Mormon 8:4–5.)

Moroni shared his testimony of the three Nephites. He and his father had both seen them, and, he wrote, "they have ministered unto us." (Verse 11.) Then with wonderful, justifiable pride, Moroni said, "I am the son of Mormon." (Verse 13.) What a blessing to be the son of such a great man! No wonder the Book of Mormon carries his name, a book that was promised to come forth in the last days:

> And it shall come in a day when the blood of saints shall cry unto the Lord, because of secret combinations and the works of darkness.
>
> Yea, it shall come in a day when the power of God shall be denied, and churches become defiled and be lifted up in the pride of their hearts; yea, even in a day when leaders of churches and teachers shall rise in the pride of their hearts, even to the envying of them who belong to their churches.
>
> Yea, it shall come in a day when there shall be heard of fires, and tempests, and vapors of smoke in foreign lands;
>
> And there shall also be heard of wars, rumors of wars, and earthquakes in divers places.
>
> Yea, it shall come in a day when there shall be great pol-

lutions upon the face of the earth; there shall be murders, and robbing, and lying, and deceivings, and whoredoms, and all manner of abominations; when there shall be many who will say, Do this, or do that, and it mattereth not, for the Lord will uphold such at the last day. But wo unto such, for they are in the gall of bitterness and in the bonds of iniquity.

Yea, it shall come in a day when there shall be churches built up that shall say: Come unto me, and for your money you shall be forgiven of your sins. (Mormon 8:27–32.)

The eighth chapter of Moroni gives us great insight concerning the prophet Mormon. In this chapter is recorded a letter that Mormon wrote to his son Moroni. The tender role of father comes out as Mormon says, "I am mindful of you always in my prayers, continually praying unto God the Father in the name of his Holy Child, Jesus, that he, through his infinite goodness and grace, will keep you through the endurance of faith on his name to the end." (Moroni 8:3.)

Later Mormon paid the supreme compliment to his son Moroni: "Behold, my son, I cannot recommend them [the Nephites] unto God lest he should smite me. But behold, my son, I recommend thee unto God, and I will trust in Christ that thou wilt be saved; and I pray unto God that he will spare thy life, to witness the return of his people unto him, or their utter destruction." (Moroni 9:21–22.)

Then Mormon counseled: "And whosoever shall believe in my name, doubting nothing, unto him will I confirm all my words, even unto the ends of the earth. And now, behold, who can stand against the works of the Lord? Who can deny his sayings? Who will rise up against the almighty power of the Lord? Who will despise the works of the Lord? Who will despise the children of Christ? Behold, all ye who are despisers of the works of the Lord, for ye shall wonder and perish." (Mormon 9:25–26.)

Mormon taught doctrine with the same forcefulness he used when leading the armies of the Nephites. For example:

Listen to the words of Christ, your Redeemer, your Lord and your God. Behold, I came into the world not to call the righteous but sinners to repentance; the whole need no physician, but they that are sick; wherefore, little children are whole, for they are not capable of committing sin; wherefore the curse of Adam is taken from them in me, that it hath no power over them; and the law of circumcision is done away in me.

And after this manner did the Holy Ghost manifest the word of God unto me; wherefore, my beloved son, I know that it is solemn mockery before God, that ye should baptize little children.

Behold I say unto you that this thing shall ye teach— repentance and baptism unto those who are accountable and capable of committing sin; yea, teach parents that they must repent and be baptized, and humble themselves as their little children, and they shall all be saved with their little children.

And their little children need no repentance, neither baptism. Behold, baptism is unto repentance to the fulfilling the commandments unto the remission of sins.

Behold I say unto you, that he that supposeth that little children need baptism is in the gall of bitterness and in the bonds of iniquity; for he hath neither faith, hope, nor charity; wherefore, should he be cut off while in the thought, he must go down to hell.

For awful is the wickedness to suppose that God saveth one child because of baptism, and the other must perish because he hath no baptism. (Moroni 8:8–11,14–15.)

And later he wrote: "And now, my beloved son, notwithstanding their hardness, let us labor diligently; for if we should cease to labor, we should be brought under condemnation; for we have a labor to perform whilst in this tabernacle of clay, that we may conquer the enemy of all righteousness, and rest our souls in the kingdom of God." (Moroni 9:6.)

Mormon died in battle. He died for a people who had no hope. The Savior said, "Greater love hath no man than this, that a man lay down his life for his friends." (John 15:13.) Mormon was filled with charity and love for his people. His life represented the greatness that few achieve.

Rudyard Kipling said:

> But there is neither East nor West,
> Border, nor Breed, nor Birth,
> When two strong men stand face to face,
> Though they come from the ends of the earth!

This is a fitting tribute to the great prophet whose name is emblazoned on every copy of the Book of Mormon. His name will stand by the side of Joseph the Prophet as a witness that the book is true.

The Savior Himself, the very Son of God, bore testimony, powerfully stating, "As your Lord and your God liveth it is true." (D&C 17:6.) The names of Joseph Smith and Mormon will be had for good and evil in the future as they have in the past. I declare with absolute truth that Joseph the Prophet and Mormon the commander-prophet have performed a work so great that it will never come to an end—no, not in all of the eternities.

## Chapter Eighteen

· · ·

## "The Last Drop in the Chalice"

Some years ago I spoke at Brigham Young University. I borrowed from Victor Hugo a title for my talk. In the book *Les Miserables,* Jean Valjean is the central figure. Near the end of the book, Victor Hugo describes the final hours of Jean Valjean's saintly life by titling the chapter "The Last Drop in the Chalice." *Les Miserables* has had a more profound influence on my life than anything else I have ever read other than the scriptures. I have read the 1,220-page translated copy five times. I will read it one or two more times, at least, before I die.

The Savior's influence is felt most directly through the lives of those who live His teachings. Many may never have known of Him or even knew they were abiding by His teachings. Nevertheless, they lived and honored the eternal truths He authored. Most who will read this book live His teachings and know Him. It is not always easy to do what He would have us do. Nor was it easy for Him to do what His Father wanted of Him. Recall that even He "would that [He] might not drink the bitter cup, and shrink—nevertheless, glory be to the Father, and [He] partook and finished [His] preparations unto the children of men." (D&C 19:18–19.) This final testing was "to finish His preparations" for us.

Many times some partake of the last drop in the chalice without any other living soul knowing or seemingly caring. When none but God can see, these faithful few still abide the most difficult trials without a thought of murmuring or self-pity. There are many heroic examples of Christ's teachings when none but God can see. Such is the story of Sandie, a little boy in Scotland, who sold matches to feed himself and his smaller brother.

"Please, sir, buy some matches!" said a little boy, with a poor thin blue face, his feet bare and red, and his clothes only a bundle of rags, although it was very cold in Edinburgh that day. "No, I don't want any," said the gentleman. "But they're only a penny a box," the little fellow pleaded. "Yes, but you see I don't want a box." "Then I'll gie ye two boxes for a penny," the boy said at last.

"And so, to get rid of him," says the gentleman, who tells the story in an English paper, "I bought a box, but then I found I had no change, so I said, 'I'll buy a box tomorrow.'

"'Oh, do buy them to-nicht,' the boy pleaded again; 'I'll rin and get ye the change; for I'm very hungry.' So I gave him the shilling, and he started away. I waited for the boy, but no boy came. Then I thought I had lost my shilling; but still there was that in the boy's face I trusted, and I did not like to think badly of him.

"Late in the evening a servant came and said a little boy wanted to see me. When the child was brought in, I found it was a smaller brother of the boy who got the shilling, but, if possible, still more ragged and thin and poor. He stood a moment diving into his rags, as if he were seeking something, and then said, 'Are you the gentleman that bought matches frae Sandie?' 'Yes.' 'Weel, then, here's fourpence oot o' yer shillin'. Sandie canna coom. He's no weel. A cart ran over him and knocked him doon; and he lost his bonnet, and his matches, and your elevenpence; and both his legs are broken, and he's no weel at a', and the doctor says he'll dee. And that's a' he can gie ye the noo,'" putting fourpence down on the table; and then the child broke down into great sobs. So I fed the little man; and then I went with him to see Sandie.

"I found that the two little things lived with a wretched drunken stepmother; their own father and mother were both dead. I found poor Sandie lying on a bundle of shavings; he knew me as soon as I came in, and said, 'I got the change, sir, and was coming back; and then the horse knocked me down, and both my legs are broken. And Reuby, little Reuby! I am sure I am deein'! And who will take care o' ye, Reuby, when I am gane? What will ye do, Reuby?'

"Then I took the poor little sufferer's hand and told him I would always take care of Reuby. He understood me, and had just strength to look at me as if he would thank me; then the expression went out of his blue eyes; and in a moment—

"'He lay within the light of God,
    Like a babe upon the breast,
Where the wicked cease from troubling,
    And the weary are at rest.'"

Heaven meant principle to that little matchboy, bruised and dying. He knew little where he was to go, but he knew better than most of those who would have spurned him from their carriages, the value of honesty, truth, nobility, sincerity, genuineness,—the qualities that go to make heaven. (*Pushing to the Front*, pp. 239–41.)

Somehow, when we hear or read an account of suffering in its purest form without complaint, without self-pity or blame, we lift to a level more near that of the incomparable Christ, He who suffered exquisitely more than man could bear and did it without a thought of self—only to do the Father's will, whatever pain or grief or suffering that might have cost. This little boy with broken legs, dying, had only two things on his heart: that a smaller brother would be taken care of and that the buyer of the matches have his change returned to him.

Marian Wright Edelman also gives us a clear picture of a teacher, Jean Thompson, who made a wonderful breakthrough as she drank from her own personal chalice and tasted the bitterness of her own conduct. Her sudden awareness dropped her to her knees, where she submitted herself to *His* loving kindness for *all* of her students:

> On the first day of school, Jean Thompson told her students, "Boys and girls, I love you all the same." Teachers lie. Little Teddy Stollard was a boy Jean Thompson did not like. He slouched in his chair, didn't pay attention, his mouth hung open in a stupor, his eyes were always unfocused, his clothes were mussed, his hair unkempt, and he smelled. He was an unattractive boy and Jean Thompson didn't like him.
>
> Teachers have records. And Jean Thompson had Teddy's. First grade: "Teddy's a good boy. He shows promise in his work and attitude. But he has a poor home situation." Second grade: "Teddy is a good boy. He does what he is told. But he is too serious. His mother is terminally ill." Third grade: "Teddy is falling behind in his work; he needs help. His mother died this year. His father shows no interest." Fourth grade: "Teddy is in deep waters; he is in need of psychiatric help. He is totally withdrawn."
>
> Christmas came, and the boys and girls brought their presents and piled them on her desk. They were all in brightly colored paper except for Teddy's. His was wrapped in brown paper and held together with scotch tape. And on it, scribbled in crayon, were the words, "For Miss Thompson from Teddy." She tore open the brown paper and out fell a rhinestone bracelet with most of the stones missing and a bottle of cheap perfume that was almost empty. When the other boys and girls began to giggle, she had enough sense to

put some of the perfume on her wrist, put on the bracelet, hold her wrist up to the children and say, "Doesn't it smell lovely? Isn't the bracelet pretty?" And taking their cue from the teacher, they all agreed.

At the end of the day, when all the children had left, Teddy lingered, came over to her desk, and said, "Miss Thompson, all day long, you smelled just like my mother. And her bracelet, that's her bracelet, it looks real nice on you, too. I'm really glad you like my presents." And when he left, she got down on her knees and buried her head in her chair and she begged God to forgive her.

The next day when the children came, she was a different teacher. She was a teacher with a heart. And she cared for all the children, but especially those who needed help. Especially Teddy. She tutored him and put herself out for him.

By the end of the year, Teddy had caught up with a lot of the children and was even ahead of some. Several years later, Jean Thompson got this note:

Dear Miss Thompson:

I'm graduating and I'm second in my high school class. I wanted you to be the first to know. Love, Teddy.

Four years later she got another note:

Dear Miss Thompson:

I wanted you to be the first to know. The university has not been easy, but I like it. Love, Teddy Stollard.

Four years later, there was another note:

Dear Miss Thompson:

As of today, I am Theodore J. Stollard, M.D. How about that? I wanted you to be the first to know. I'm going to be married in July. I want you to come and sit where my mother would have sat, because you're the only family I have. Dad died last year.

And she went and she sat where his mother should have sat because she deserved to be there. (Deval L. Patrick in *Vital Speeches*, 1994, p. 93.)

One wonders at the profound impact some seemingly insignificant acts we perform have. A good deed is never lost, however insignificant or obscure it might be. The wonderful contribution of a mite to the church's treasury does not go unnoticed. There are many acts of mercy and tenderness, many words of compassion and consolation, many gifts of heart and soul that none but God can see. Nevertheless, He does see; He does know; and He, I am certain, is tenderly, sincerely, sweetly grateful to those who give them. This whole life is about service—service in its purest form; service performed to bless and lift our fellow beings; service that seeks no reward except making someone's burden lighter or bringing a moment of relief. And so many marvelous, wonderful, Christ-like deeds are done where no eye can see, no ear can hear, and no one will ever know.

Many Saints live honorable lives of great integrity. They work hard every day of their lives, they serve faithfully in whatever way they can, and they raise sweet and wonderful families. Theirs may be an inconspicuous contribution, but nonetheless they will merit eternal life and exaltation as they comply with the Savior's holy commands.

In chapter 2 we dealt with the part of the Atonement that covers the "suffering pains and afflictions and temptations *of every kind;* . . . he will take upon him their infirmities, that his bowels may be filled with mercy . . . , that he may know according to the flesh how to succor his people according to their infirmities." (Alma 7:11–12; emphasis added.) There is a principle in these verses that few understand. We take upon ourselves the infirmities of others that our bowels may be filled with mercy. "Blessed are the merciful: for they shall obtain mercy." (Matthew 5:7.) What a glorious promise! We also learn how to succor His people. We learn much through empathy and love: we learn how to succor and to have our bowels filled with mercy.

As we walk through life, we influence many people. We model what they see every day. A slightly dishonest act, an unkind word, a loss of temper, a profane outburst, a white lie, a thoughtless act—all provide an image of what we really are. The reverse is also true. Every sweet and tender act we perform—our happy, buoyant spirit; the way we treat our children and our spouse; and the daily code of Christian conduct we perform—all provide the beholder with an image of us.

It is a wonderful goal in life to improve our personal life, to strengthen our virtues, to overcome our weaknesses, and to be ever growing upward to Christ's standards. There is a consequence for good or ill of everything we do. "The last drop in the chalice" suggests there may be at least one more trial in life, one more opportunity left to prove who we really are and what kind of an impact we have had on others.

I subscribe to a publication called *Vital Speeches.* Over the years I occasionally have come across speeches by E. Grady Bogue. In my humble opinion, he is a teacher with a capital T. In a speech he gave in 1988 he said:

> Rightly done, teaching is a precious work. It is, however, the one human endeavor most damaging in consequence when done without care or competence. To carry a student in harm's way because of either ignorance or arrogance— because we do not know or do not care—is an act far worse than a bungled surgery. Our mistakes will not bleed. Instead, they carry hidden scars whose mean and tragic consequences may not be seen until years have passed and remedy is painful and impossible. (*Vital Speeches,* 1988, p. 615.)

One thing "the last drop in the chalice" suggests is that we will be held accountable for our conduct and the influence we have had on the lives of others. The earlier in life we commit to follow the Master's divine direction, the fewer drops of sourness there will be in our chalice.

A young couple came to my office. The husband was a sweet, committed Latter-day Saint. He was a returned missionary and a very bright young father. He had extremely impressive credentials. I interviewed him for worthiness as a potential employee in the

Church educational system. I asked the wife if he was a good husband, if they got along, and how he treated her. She responded in a passive way. I then asked if she could support him in his calling, his schooling, and his employment. Hesitatingly, she said she thought she could support him, although he wasn't home very much. He was a stake executive secretary, he was writing his dissertation, and he was earning a living. I could read her thoughts: being home with the three little children and a busy husband. I said, "You didn't marry a normal man, a man who goes to work and is off at five and is home every evening. You married a very special man who has wonderful and great things to do and become. He will make you terribly proud of him. The Lord has special things for him to do, and you will be equal to him in all he does. You will need to come to understand that it really is better to have a reduced quantity of time with a very high-quality man than a great quantity of time from a lesser-quality individual." Great men and great women have learned how to put quality into whatever they do, including relationships with family members. This may be a test for this wonderful woman, but by and by she will see the blessing in it.

The last drop in the chalice is not necessarily the greatest test we will face in life. President Harold B. Lee stated that we would be tested every month of our lives. As we are able to modify our perspective of "tests" when they come, we meet them knowing that we will be the beneficiaries in some way.

If you could have the power to determine what your final test in life would be, what would you choose? Consider such tests as terminal illness, lingering illness, financial disaster, wayward children, conflict with other Church members, surgery, a loss of one or more of the five senses, or an unfaithful companion. I think we would not choose to involve others; rather we would make our test one that spared our loved ones. However, we ought to be prepared for whatever testing may come. I believe that part of being properly prepared is remembering that Christ took upon himself our pains, sicknesses, infirmities, afflictions, and trials. He offers us solace and assistance if we will but ask and then accept it.

Certain scriptures can bring us comfort and understanding. In Leviticus we read, "The life of the flesh is in the blood: and I have given it to you upon the altar to make an atonement for your souls: for it is the blood that maketh an atonement for the soul." (Leviticus 17:11.) We do not understand the fulness of the Atonement, the most glorious and pivotal act ever performed by the Lord, but somehow we know that "the Lord hath laid on him the iniquity of us all." (Isaiah 53:6.)

The Master has promised great blessings to those who minister to His children in whatever way they can:

> And he shall set the sheep on his right hand, but the goats on the left.
>
> Then shall the King say unto them on his right hand, Come, ye blessed of my Father, inherit the kingdom prepared for you from the foundation of the world:
>
> For I was an hungred, and ye gave me meat: I was thirsty, and ye gave me drink: I was a stranger, and ye took me in:
>
> Naked, and ye clothed me: I was sick, and ye visited me: I was in prison, and ye came unto me.
>
> Then shall the righteous answer him, saying, Lord, when saw we thee an hungred, and fed thee? or thirsty, and gave thee drink?
>
> When saw we thee a stranger, and took thee in? or naked, and clothed thee?
>
> Or when saw we thee sick, or in prison, and came unto thee?
>
> And the King shall answer and say unto them, Verily I say unto you, Inasmuch as ye have done it unto one of the least of these my brethren, ye have done it unto me. (Matthew 25:33–40.)

It is my belief that those who serve others do increase their ability to empathize. Their bowels are filled with mercy and love. Their spirits soften and modify because they model the teachings of the Master, and truly He will gather them on His right hand.

Let me share several quotations with you about adversity. They are taken from the book *A New Dictionary of Quotations,* compiled by H. L. Mencken. You will find a common thread running through them.

- "Prosperity getteth friends, but adversity trieth them." (Nicholas Ling Politeuphia, 1597.)
- "A man hath many enemies when his back is to the wall." (John Clarke, Paroemiologia Anglo-Latina, 1639.)
- "In time of prosperity friends will be plenty; In time of adversity not one in twenty." (James Howell; Proverbs 1659.)
- "Adversity introduces a man to himself." (Author unidentified.)

Oftentimes we feel alone when adversity comes. We might even see those whom we supposed were dear friends avoid or abandon us. We may suffer in silence and endure alone.

Oliver Goldsmith said: "The greatest object in the universe, is a good person struggling with adversity; yet there is a still greater, which is the good person that comes to relieve it." (*The Vicar of Wakefield.*)

The wonderful thing about the Atonement is that we need not feel that we suffer alone or that we are ever abandoned if we live right. The Atonement provides an Advocate who has suffered for our afflictions, illnesses, and pains. We cannot face any trial or testing in this life that He has not vicariously suffered more than all of us collectively. He will never leave us. He was the best man ever to walk on the face of this earth. He did more good than any other. He exemplified greater humility, more tenderness, and deeper charity than anyone else who ever lived. He alone understands the fulness of the trials we face as we drink the last drop in the chalice, and He alone will stand supreme to comfort, bless, and abide with us during our darkest hours. He is the light of the world. He is not only the Son of God, He is God; and I so testify.

# INDEX

. . .

Index